Entertaining
at the
College of Charleston

Entertaining
at the
College of Charleston

by

Zoe D. Sanders

Enjoy!
Zoe Sanders

Photography by William Struhs
Project Consultant Marion Sullivan

The College of Charleston Foundation

Manufactured in Hong Kong

Library of Congress Cataloging-in-Publication Data

Sanders, Zoe D., 1938-
Entertaining at the College of Charleston / by Zoe D. Sanders;
photography by William Struhs; project consultant, Marion Sullivan.
p.   cm.
Includes index.
ISBN 0-9638620-1-4
1. Entertaining. 2. Cookery. 3. Menus. 4. College of
Charleston. I. College of Charleston. II. Title.
TX731.S295 1998
642′ .4 -- dc21   98-34652
CIP

Contents

INTRODUCTION BY PAT CONROY, vii

FOREWORD BY ANNE RIVERS SIDDONS, xi

PREFACE, xiii

ACKNOWLEDGMENTS, xv

DEDICATION, xvii

TIPS FOR SUCCESS WITH THESE RECIPES, xix

MENUS

FOUNDATION DINNER, THE BLACKLOCK HOUSE, 1

RECEPTION AFTER THE PERFORMANCE, SOTTILE THEATER, 7

COUGAR CLUB PARTY, REMLEY'S POINT, 11

THE ROUND TABLE, RANDOLPH HALL, 17

FALL OYSTER ROAST AND PIG PICKING, DIXIE PLANTATION, 23

PARENTS WEEKEND, THE CISTERN, 29

EQUESTRIAN TEAM BRUNCH, STORYBOOK FARM, 35

BOARD OF TRUSTEES LUNCH, THE PRESIDENT'S BOARD ROOM, RANDOLPH HALL, 41

ALUMNI DINNER, SIMONS CENTER FOR HISTORIC PRESERVATION, 45

Mid-Winter Graduation Speakers Luncheon, The President's House, 51

Holiday Drop-In, The President's House, 57

Simons Guild Holiday Luncheon, The Garden Room, The President's House, 63

Faculty & Staff Holiday Party, Willard A. Silcox Gymnasium, 67

New Year's Day Dinner, The Kitchen, The President's House, 73

Academic Affairs Breakfast, Faculty House, 79

School of the Arts Dinner, Faculty House, 83

Donors Celebration, The President's House, 89

Dessert in the Kathleen K. Lightsey Garden, Randolph Hall, 97

Sailing Team Snacks, Charleston Harbor, 101

Spring Graduation Speakers Luncheon, 105

Graduation Reception, Courtyard, The President's House, 109

Spoleto Supper, Garden Room, The President's House, 113

Avery Research Center Gala Dinner, The Avery Institute, 119

Foundation Lunch, Board Room, The Sottile House, 125

Additional Recipes, 131

Guide to Illustrations, 149

Index, 153

Introduction
by
Pat Conroy

At the very first moment when I first met Alex Sanders, the mythical and larger-than-life President of the College of Charleston, it was on a hillside in North Georgia where he stood holding a brace of live Maine lobsters in a doughnut box while he taught a group of children a magic trick. We were the guests of two ebullient Georgians, Joe and Emily Cumming, on the first of twenty-five annual weekends when a specially selected group of friends would gather for sparkling conversation and superb food. I had always thought I had a good personality until I met Alex Sanders, and I found myself gripped by a kind of autism during that memorable encounter when Alex dazzled the entire entourage with stories about the South that seemed epical in scope and definitive in nature. But we met at sunset with the long shadows moving across the hills, and the last light sliding across the mountain lake like icing slow to cool.

Emily Cumming, our hostess, pointed toward the disappearing sun and shouted to her musical and sometimes over-theatrical family, "Oh, look. The sunset. The sheer Beauty of the world."

Her husband, Joe, a wordsmith of great note, added, "By God, this light is a changeling, even a barbaric thing. Thus, this noble orb, engorged with mercury and gold, vanishes even as we speak the name of harsh, demonic night...."

I was new to all this and found it interesting, indeed. Long prepared for these sudden, pagan-like moments of ecstasy, the four Cumming children from eight to eighteen rushed to their parents' side and all six of them began humming, tuning, and harmonizing their voices, sounding much like musical instruments warming up in an orchestra pit.

Alex Sanders and his wife, Zoe, watched my reaction to all this with great bemusement. I saw Alex smile as my face turned to pure astonishment when the Cumming family bade farewell to the fast disappearing sun by bursting into song, two altos, two baritones...I would like to say two eunuchs, but you get the picture:

"Day is done, yes, the day is done.
Day is done
Yes, oh Lord, day is done."

I am not speaking here of a shy, Trappist-like praise of the spilling of time as in Lauds or Matins. It looked like the finale of "Showboat" or "West Side Story" with everyone singing at the top of their voices, their arms extended, Joe down on one knee, and Emily thrusting an umbrella out toward the mountains and beyond.

Alex Sanders noticed my puzzlement and utter surprise at the suddenness and spontaneity of the scene as the valley rang with the echoes of the hymn.

Then, Alex spoke. "Ah! I could not help but notice–this is your first time with the Family Von Trapp."

I fell in love with Alex Sanders that weekend and I was simply one of the many over the years who have been overwhelmed and ambushed in the field by the sheer immensity of his charm. By a roaring fire on the second day, Alex told two of the greatest stories I had ever heard in my life, and I had to fight the urge to retreat to my room to record them in my journal while their fresh, persimmon-like details still burned along the taste buds of memory. In firelight, he had the head of a Javanese tiger and a serenity that enabled him to hold court without resorting to coarseness or testosterone. He waited his turn, then used a matador's skill in controlling the pace of his narrative; and by changing the rhythm of his great accented voice, he could move us the way the matador could change the direction of a bull's charge by the flick of the wrist and the false billow created in that acreage of red cape. His phrasing was eloquent, colloquial, and his pitch was perfect. Wonderful writers surrounded him and all of them found themselves bested and awed.

That weekend changed my life and I will always remember Alex sitting in his flannel shirt with the smell of burning wood around us as the fires of autumn lit up the ridge of Tate Mountain with the surprising beauty that withering grants to its high forests. Alex's stories matched the uncommon colors of fall where the trees flared up in all the vividness of wild roses gone to seed, the wings of hair-streaks and hummingbirds and all the last rainbows of the dying year. Never had I encountered stories so original, so strong with delightful detail, so perfect. Like woodsmoke, his stories were born of fire, then carried away through air.

All this I mention in regard to the publication of this extraordinary cookbook. Whenever I have been in the presence of Zoe and Alex Sanders in my lifetime, the food has always been fabulous, the company nonpareil, the drink free-flowing and plentiful, and the conversation thrilling, heady, and life-changing. As a couple, they have turned the dailiness of life into an art form and invited anyone who crosses their path to learn all its steps and secrets. As the College of Charleston now knows, President and Mrs. Sanders live out their lives at full speed and they are incapable of holding anything back. Both of them are two of the finest cooks I have ever met in my life, and I have eaten like a deposed Italian king when I've found myself a lucky guest in their house. Both know well the pleasure and tenderness and satisfaction that a well-composed meal can bring to its happy guests.

Once, I sat with friends as Alex and Zoe fixed a fish stew that I remember being far superior to any bouillabaisse that I ordered in the back streets of Marseilles. The rouille they composed to top that soup in cloud-like dollops was a love song to garlic. I can summon up visions of past meals that have included ice chests loaded down with shrimp that had been swimming offshore that morning; oysters gathered during the last low tide; salads glistening with olive oil and darkened with raindrops of balsamic vinegar; fennel and red peppers blistered on the same grills where the marinated flank steaks will follow; quail and wild rice swimming in gravy; sirloin steaks, as large as my head, hanging off serving platters; grouper and salmon and mahimahi coming off their bones in nuggets of white flesh that tastes like seaborne butter to the palate.

You can eat better at the table of Zoe and Alex Sanders than you have any right to eat at any table on earth. Like me, they are amateur cooks and these recipes can be mastered easily by anyone who can read passingly well and has even an ounce of passion for food. Zoe Sanders has as inimitable a reputation and mystique as a hostess, as her husband does as an orator or storyteller or judge or educator. She is pretty, fiercely competent, fiery in her beliefs and tenacious in her loves and enthusiasms. This cookbook is one of her loves.

Both Alex Sanders and I have been accused of being prone to grotesque exaggeration in our careers, and there is great merit when that accusation is directed at Alex. But in my own defense, I can never convince people outside the South that I know someone as pointlessly colorful, outrageous, bone-jarringly amusing and pixilated as Alex Sanders himself. Alex helped me understand that the South I grew up in is so over-the-top and over-baked that I see myself as a shy minimalist trying to ink black-and-white woodcuts of my native land. Southerners all know that the South is too bizarre and out-of-control for its own good. I always find myself having to surrender some of the juice, hold back on the cayenne and Tabasco, for the sake of credibility itself.

When *The Prince of Tides* came out in 1986, I sat in the Four Seasons Restaurant in New York answering questions from a hostile reporter. I never thought I would be conducting much of this interview about Alex Sanders while I dined on sweetbreads poached in white wine, while a journalist skewered my brightest work.

"I found the white porpoise scene in your novel a little much," she said, toying with her salad. Critics are mostly bulimic, rail-thin—no great appetites there. "Homage to Herman Melville. Right?"

"Wrong," I said. "Alex Sanders told me the story."

"Who is Alex Sanders?" she asked.

"The Greatest of all South Carolinians," I answered. "I thanked him in the acknowledgments."

"You thanked everyone in the acknowledgments," she said. "But there's no white porpoise, right?"

"Wrong. I saw the White Porpoise swimming in Harbor River when I was at Beaufort High School."

I could tell she did not believe me, but she went on with the next question. "In your book you have a Bengal tiger at a gas station. How ridiculous."

"I'm sorry," I say, eating happily. "Another story from Alex Sanders. That was Happy the Tiger at an Esso gas station on Gervais Street in Columbia. I once fed Happy a chicken neck after I got my car washed."

Let's go on," she said, her voice skeptical.

"The moving of the town? To make way for a plutonium plant?"

"Want to go to the town?" I asked. "It's called New Ellenton."

"You claim it's true."

"I could get you a radiation burn at the plant, if you're so inclined."

She looked over her notes, then said, "And you're going to tell me Alex Sanders told you this story."

"It's one of his best," I said.

"Do you pay Alex Sanders royalties?" she asked.

"If I were a good and decent man, I certainly would. But I prefer to simply rob him of all his material and take full credit for it. He does the same to me."

"Do you ever have any ideas of your own?" she asked scornfully.

"Every once in a while I borrow from my own meager pantry of ideas. But not often."

"What does this Alex Sanders do? Is he employed?" she asked.

"He's the Chief Justice of South Carolina's Court of Appeals, and teaches at Harvard Law School."

She studied me for a moment, then said, "You're exaggerating again."

"Hot shot reporter like yourself could find out in a jif," I said, my voice revealing my irritation.

"You sound hostile."

"You find me dishonest."

"I'm skeptical," she said.

"That makes me hostile."

"Does the great Alex Sanders find you hostile?"

"He finds me perfectly delightful in every possible way," I said.

"Why?" she asked.

"Because, I feel exactly the same way about him. I'd rather spend an evening with Alex Sanders than anyone I've ever met. You'd feel exactly the same way if you knew Alex. Everyone does."

Again, her eyes went to her notes, and her

hostility was like a condiment to the meal. She said, "Let's go to the old chestnut. If you could invite any three people in history to a dinner party, who would they be?"

"Alex Sanders. Alex Sanders. Then Alex Sanders again."

"You're making fun of the question," she said.

"I certainly am. You want me to answer Jesus of Nazareth, Genghis Khan and Eva Braun. Something like that."

"Something like that," she said, then she looked around at the decor of the unsurpass-able Four Seasons. "Why did you want to eat in a place like this? I find it pretentious."

"It was recommended to me by Alex Sanders and his lovely wife, Zoe."

The reporter rose up to shake my hand and said, in parting, "I haven't believed a word you've said."

I found this strange encounter in one of my journals and wanted to include it in this introduction because Zoe and Alex are unlike any two people I have ever met. They have entered my life like two sharply-tanged sorbets, coming in the middle of meals to cleanse the palate and ready you for the feast that is on its way from the kitchen. Always, they have surprised me with their uncanny and inex-haustible generosity: This book is an expression of their genius for friendship. In this cookbook you will find a saucier's love of herbs, and a food lover's willingness to try almost anything. Many recipes will have a bit-ing piquancy, the astringency of citrus and vinegar, the tear-stained presence of jalapeno and horseradish. But there is also the residue of brine and the surprising sweetness that can be coaxed out of honeycombs, orange groves, blueberries and mangoes.

By inviting Alex and Zoe Sanders into their community, The College of Charleston made the whole city a better place to be. Meeting them changed my life forever and I could not be more grateful to them. Now, Zoe Sanders has put her prodigious talent for cooking and entertaining into this one exqui-sitely wrought volume that will provide schol-arships for students of the College.

By purchasing this book, your life will be fuller, richer, deeper—and much, much better fed. It adds to the revolution that has taken place in the world of food and cuisine in Charleston in the last ten years. All colleges and cookbooks exist because of an unutterable hunger we all carry into the night. We look for texts like this one to sustain and feed and show us how to live with purpose and brio and great, great joy.

Foreword
by
Anne Rivers Siddons

The College of Charleston was founded in 1770 and chartered in 1785. It is the oldest municipal college in this country. It is and always has been a strong liberal arts college. Ten thousand students come here, and are taught by a faculty of 400 plus.

These are the facts and they are for the mind to know. Ah, but the heart knows the truth of the matter: that the College is a magical place, inalterably woven into the fabric of this enchanting city and the Lowcountry around it. Hauntingly beautiful in all its aspects and seasons; drowned in seas of flowers in the springs; sunk deep in the long, dreaming, moss shaded summers; burning in the slow, golden autumns that light the sunsets to wildfire; drifting in the soft winters when the mists off the rivers and marshes wrap the campus in mystery.

Who knows who—or what—you might meet in the twilight fog on the paths around the Cistern? Who knows if the footsteps just beyond the range of the gaslights are of this time or another? In a place where the Department of Philosophy is housed in a century-old cottage that looks for all the world as if, inside, someone still seeks the formula for turning base metal into gold, anything is possible.

The College's central commitment may be, and properly so, to the future, but the past glides one scant step behind it always. Like the Lowcountry itself, the College of Charleston is a place of ritual, tradition, fetes and feasts. In the Lowcountry the stomach knows the truth of the matter, too. This region has been blessed with abundant riches from the water and the earth, and sometimes the sky, and the College gratefully uses them all in its many annual celebrations: oysters, crabs, shrimp, sweet-fleshed fish; doves, venison, ducks; rice, sweet potatoes, benne seeds, grits; sun-ripened vegetables that grow almost the year through.

All over the campus, at all times of the year, at parties large and small, you can sample the bounty of the Lowcountry: outdoors, under the old oaks in the spring, banked in flowers; beside the slow rivers and green marshes in summer, spilling from picnic baskets; in high-ceilinged dining rooms in the fall, candlelight flickering on old silver and china fashioned in another century; by firelight in the winter, the thousand lights of December dancing in every goblet.

For those of you who have dined at a College feast, this book will be a chance both to remember and to recreate some of the magic. For those who have not, it's a way to share the special sorcery of a place that is like no other on earth.

I get to say all these extravagant things because I am not of the College, and therefore cannot be accused of partisan ravings. And besides, everybody knows novelists are bad to carry on. But I have been a guest at various tables here, and have always been enthralled by Charleston and the Lowcountry, and I know good things when I taste them. This book is full of them.

So get cracking. It's almost suppertime.

Preface

Entertaining began for me in 1942 when I fascinated Alex Sanders by popping roly-poly bugs in my mouth and down my throat when we were in the four-year-old class at Rose Hill Kindergarten in Columbia, South Carolina. I continued to entertain him during our courting days in the early sixties by showing off my shotgun expertise at skeet shooting. He in turn courted me by preparing and serving romantic four- and five-course delectable meals by candlelight with his mother's china and silver and his father's recipes (plus a few of his own). I was as completely enamored of his entertaining skills as he was with my shooting skills, and we were married in 1964. Our daughter, Zoe Caroline, was born in 1967.

Until 1982 our way of life was shaped by my involvement in animal rights and cruelty prevention, Zoe Caroline's determination to be a straight "A" student, and Alex's law practice, teaching, and political campaigns (with their barbecues and fish fries). Then I decided to go to work as the Kitchen Coordinator at our church, Trinity Episcopal Cathedral. I had in the meantime found out that Alex was an excellent shot, and I had begun to discover that I could cook.

My job was to coordinate volunteers as we prepared and served meals with fresh seasonal food for the parishioners, the elderly, the homeless, and hundreds of people who needed a place to meet and eat. We served an average of 1,200 meals a month and held receptions for multitudes of people from through-out the diocese. In 1988 I accepted a similar position with Trenholm Road United Methodist Church, where we served even larger numbers of people from all over South Carolina – and I continued to add to and perfect my collection of recipes and menus.

In 1991 Alex, who had been Chief Judge of the South Carolina Court of Appeals for nine years, began to consider a career change. In October of the following year we moved into the Bishop Robert Smith House (c. 1770) at 6 Glebe Street in Charleston, the home of the President of the College of Charleston.

The College, one of the original colonial colleges and the 13th oldest in the nation, was founded in 1770 and has an enrollment of 10,000 students. Three signers of the Declaration of Independence and three men who helped draft the Constitution of the United States have served on its Board of Trustees.

My first responsibility was to have many small dinner parties of no more than 20 people for friends and supporters of the College. The Bishop Robert Smith House and its gardens have provided a spectacular setting for dinners and receptions for up to 500 people, including the 1994 wedding of Zoe Caroline and William Norman Nettles. (Five hundred people are more than the average enrollment during the first 150 years of the College's existence!) As you peruse this book, you will see photographs of many of the places where small as well as large groups gather in the 18th- and 19th-century houses on the campus. These magically charming and deceptively functional old buildings house classes, dormitory rooms, and professors' offices.

When I walk into a spacious ballroom on the second floor of a private home in Charleston, I am reminded of how elaborate entertaining was in the city's early years. As a port city, Charleston had access to a larger and more varied selection of food and wines than other areas of South Carolina. Eliza Pinckney put together a small collection of "receipts," as Charlestonians refer to recipes, as early as 1756.

My goal has been for the College to live up to Charleston's fine and rich culinary heritage of entertaining. The menus and recipes in this book are perhaps better suited for entertaining than they are for a steady diet. They are rich in fat and salt, the ingredients that make food taste good. (However, if I were a dietician in a nursing home or fed my family three meals a day, I would use most of these recipes—but with adjustments in fat and salt.)

With few exceptions, the most inexperienced cook can, in the proper season, suc-

cessfully produce these meals. The ingredients are readily available at larger grocery stores, and the spices are generally found on your spice shelf. I am not a gourmet cook, but I do like good food.

Most of the seafood, vegetables, flowers, and fruit are local and are found offshore, on the islands, on the campus, or in private gardens in the city. Musical performances by our talented students and professors in the School of the Arts provide entertainment at most of our events.

The College of Charleston has provided Alex and me with a life steeped in traditions and rich in social and cultural experiences in an historic setting of antique beauty. In years to come we plan to retire on nearby rural Wadmalaw Island and continue to take advantage of all the City and the College have to offer. This institution will invigorate and rejuvenate the mind, the body, and the spirit of both the young and the old who choose to spend time in this extraordinary place.

Zoe and Alex, at age 4, in their kindergarten photograph

Acknowledgments

Thank you to ARAMARK Campus Services and Bill Carswell for their support of the book and to the ARAMARK staff; Catering Chef, Lee Godbey; Managers José Tortolero, Patrick Duddy, Ken Gneiting, Tara Guérard, David Janecek, and William Catoe; Food Consultant, Marion Sullivan; Creative Designer, Terry Hawkins; Food Service Attendants Irene Wilson, Willette Watson, Kenny Geddis, and the many students who work part-time. This wonderful crew makes entertaining pure pleasure for me.

To the College of Charleston Foundation, the Board of Trustees, Rab Finlay, Jane Turner, Doris Meddin, Ann Purcell, Josephine Abney, Jane Avinger, Margaret Sheldon, and Jack Tate for their support and confidence in me.

To Peggy Ashby, Bridget Hindman, Myrna Barkoot, and Glenn Deleston for keeping the President's House running smoothly in spite of the many disruptions.

To Adèle and Fraser Wilson, Lisa and Fraser Wilson, Jr., Dottie Jordan, Janie Thornhill, Lucia Childs, Elaine and Jack Folline, Marion Sullivan, Mary Ellen Long Way, Joyce Long Darby, Marty Whaley Adams, Theodora and Albert Simons, and Frances Harvey Morris for sharing and in many instances donating their antique silver, porcelain, linens, furniture, portraits, prints, and personal treasures for entertaining at the College and for the pictures taken for the book.

To Sally Simons, Lawrence Walker, Barbara Stine, Louise Bennett, Townie Krawcheck, Martha and Fletcher Derrick, Andrea Limehouse, Louisa Prichard Hawkins, Eleanor and Earl Kline, Mimi and Koichiro Hirao for many of the beautiful flowers and fruit seen in the photographs.

To Marty Whaley Adams for arranging the flowers pictured on the cover and Bridget Hindman, Marion Sullivan, and Terry Hawkins for arranging the flowers and creative decorations seen throughout the book.

To the College Alumni Association and the Young Alumni Association for their enthusiasm and support.

To Bob Story at Storybook Farm for helping with the equestrian shot.

To coaches George Wood, Colin Bentley and Stephen Sparkman and to sailing students Harcourt Schutz, Jon Colarusso, Cory Vietor, and Alan Uram for the sailing shot and to Stanley Woerth for the use of his boat.

To John Kresse and the entire basketball team and all of the other athletic teams for making me proud.

To Jim Shumate and the College Physical Plant employees; Paty Cowden and the Grounds Department; and Major James Parlor and the Public Safety Officers for assisting us in every way possible.

To Nan Morrison, whom I consider my "personal editor."

To Jane Iseley, Heyward Siddons, Carolyn Krupp, John Wilson, and Susan Hunter for their valuable advice on how to write and get a book published.

To Betsy Williams, Ann Cotton, and Sarah Fox for difficult proofreading.

To Pat Jablonsky Ring, Terry Richardson, Susie Martin, and Tommy Thompson for their generous contributions of photographs.

To Bill Struhs, who took spectacular pictures and many more that we didn't have room to use.

To Pete and Connie Wyrick, Charles Cornwell, and Simons Young for professionally, beautifully, and efficiently publishing the book.

To Robert Dickson, Lee Godbey, and Bridget Hindman for advice, help, and sharing in "tasting" and testing recipes.

To Ben Moise, Jim Quinn, and my husband for their special recipe contributions.

To Raven Graydon and the Trinity Episcopal Cathedral Kitchen Volunteers and the Trenholm Road United Methodist Church Food Brood, who shared their recipes and helped me develop them for the multitudes; and all of the wonderful cooks who have given me their recipes over the years.

To Nathalie Dupree for her advice, encouragement, and accolades.

To Pat Conroy for his support and help in the beginning and for his grand introduction and confirmation that Alex "did" tell him many of his stories for *The Prince of Tides*.

To Anne Rivers Siddons for her beautiful description of the College of Charleston in the Foreword.

To Marion Sullivan, who has been mentioned for many contributions, but the most important one for me was to keep me organized and make me get it done.

I am eternally grateful to you all.

Dedicated To

the Kitchen Volunteers
at Trinity Episcopal Cathedral
and Trenholm Road United Methodist Church,
who made hard work fun;

the thousands of appreciative people
who challenged and inspired me to produce
a variety of menus and recipes;

Zoe Caroline,
who had the patience to wait until
the soup for two thousand was served before she got hers;

Bill Nettles,
who loves my food;

Alex,
who taught me to cook;

Adèle and Fraser Wilson,
who taught me to appreciate and understand
the beauty in the Charleston way of life;

and
The College of Charleston Community,
for which this book is written.

Tips for Success with These Recipes

Read the entire recipe several hours before cooking in order to set out the necessary room temperature ingredients.

All pans are measured across the top, not the bottom.

All milk is whole milk unless otherwise noted.

All herbs are dried unless otherwise noted.

All butter is salted unless otherwise noted.

All sugar is granulated white unless otherwise noted.

All eggs are Grade A Large.

All mushrooms are white, "button" mushrooms.

Finely ground pepper incorporates evenly in cooked foods.

Celery *stalks* are made up of individual *ribs*.

Oyster liquor is the natural juice that an oyster has in its shell.

Fresh lemon juice prevents sliced avocados and apples from turning brown.

Large amounts of cooked tomatoes will sour and ferment if not transferred to a cool container and refrigerated, partially covered, immediately after cooking.

To "process" means to use an electric food processor with a sharp blade or an electric blender.

When inserting a testing thermometer for doneness, be sure to insert it into the thickest place without touching bone or bottom of pan.

The "zest" of citrus fruit is the thin, colored outer layers of the rind containing the flavor of the citrus oils. Underneath zest is the bitter white part of the rind called the pith. When using a "grater" or "zester," avoid taking any of the white pith.

Most thin-skinned fruits and vegetables peel easily when dipped into boiling water for 1 minute.

To prepare hard-boiled eggs, cover eggs with cold water and cook uncovered for 30 minutes on medium low. (They should gently bubble and steam but never reach a boil.) Cool with cold water and peel.

A southern-style breakfast in the courtyard overlooking Porter's Lodge

Foundation Dinner
The Blacklock House

CRAB SALAD

ROUND TABLE GRILLED VEAL CHOPS
SCALLOPED POTATOES
SAUTÉED FRESH SPINACH AND LEEKS
COLLEGE BISCUITS

SWEDISH CREAM
WITH
RASPBERRY SAUCE

ICED TEA
RED AND WHITE WINE
COFFEE

Crab Salad

Lobster meat from 4 one-pound lobsters can be substituted for crab to make an elegant first course for dinner.

8 first-course servings

2 large bunches watercress, long stems removed
2 pounds fresh jumbo lump crab meat, gently picked over for shells
16 very thin slivers sweet red pepper for garnish

Dressing
⅔ cup Hellmann's® mayonnaise
2 Tablespoons ketchup
1 teaspoon cognac
1 Tablespoon + 2 teaspoons fresh lemon juice
½ teaspoon curry powder
Pinch salt
Pinch cayenne pepper
½ teaspoon finely minced mild onion

Combine mayonnaise, ketchup, cognac, lemon juice, curry powder, salt, and cayenne. Refrigerate until ready to serve. Add onion just before serving.

TO ASSEMBLE: Make bed of watercress on 8 salad plates. Place ¼ pound crab meat in center of watercress. Drizzle dressing over crab. Garnish with 2 thin slivers of red pepper.

Round Table Grilled Veal Chops

Alex suggests that you ask your butcher for center-cut chops with the largest tenderloin possible.

Serves 8

8 center-cut veal chops, 1 ½-inches thick
2 teaspoons salt
2 teaspoons black pepper

Sprinkle each chop with salt and pepper. Cook over very hot charcoal until chops reach desired degree of doneness (approximately 6-7 minutes on each side for medium rare).

Scalloped Potatoes

Serves 8

5 Tablespoons butter, melted
3 large cloves fresh garlic, peeled and pressed
3 pounds baking potatoes
1 teaspoon salt
1 teaspoon black pepper
6 Tablespoons chopped fresh chives
2 cups (8 ounces) grated Swiss Cheese
1 cup half-and-half

2-quart (3-inch deep) baking dish

Preheat oven to 425°. Brush baking dish with 1 Tablespoon butter.

Heat remaining 4 Tablespoons butter on medium and sauté pressed garlic until soft and beginning to turn light brown.

Peel potatoes and drop in cold water. Cut ⅛-inch slices one layer at a time as you layer the dish. Do NOT slice ahead and place in water. As you layer potatoes, drizzle a third of the butter and garlic over them and spread it out with your fingertips. Sprinkle the layers with a third of the salt, pepper, chives and cheese. Pour a third of the half-and-half over them. Repeat twice.

Cover dish tightly with aluminum foil and bake at 425° for 45 minutes. Remove foil. Bake 15 minutes, or until potatoes are tender when pierced with fork and top is golden brown.

Sautéed Fresh Spinach and Leeks

Serves 8

2 ½ pounds fresh spinach, stems removed
1 cup julienned leeks, white only
1 stick butter
1 ½ teaspoons salt

3-gallon pot with lid

Drop spinach leaves in sink filled with cold water. Shake leaves in water, allowing dirt, sand, and trash to fall to bottom. Remove spinach, drain sink, and wash again. Take leaves by handfuls, shake off water, and place in colander.

Trim leeks down to white part. (The green is too tough.) Split leeks down middle and wash well between layers to remove dirt. Julienne leeks by cutting into very thin uniform strips.

Heat butter in pot on medium. Add leeks and sauté 2 minutes, or until tender. Add spinach and sprinkle with salt, tossing to combine with leeks. Cover pot and cook spinach 6 to 8 minutes, stirring occasionally. Do not add any water; spinach cooks in its own juices. Drain and serve spinach as soon as possible after cooking. It turns "Charleston green" (black with a hint of green) when held hot in its own juices longer than 20 minutes before serving.

Sautéed Fresh Spinach

Serves 8

3 pounds fresh spinach, stems removed
1 ½ teaspoons salt
¾ stick butter

3-gallon pot with lid

Wash spinach as described above. Put wet spinach in pot. Do not add water; spinach will cook in its own juices. Sprinkle with salt, cover, and cook on medium 6 to 8 minutes, stirring occasionally. Drain. Melt butter and add to spinach. Toss and serve.

College Biscuits

Frances Harvey Chalk Morris (Mrs. James A.) of Columbia taught us how to make these biscuits at Trinity Cathedral. I have taught hundreds of people to make them since then. A light touch is the key to good biscuits.

24 (2-inch) biscuits or 32 (1 ½ -inch) party biscuits

2 cups self-rising flour
1 ½ teaspoons sugar
¾ cup Crisco® Butter Flavor shortening
¾ cup buttermilk
½ cup (2 ounces) grated extra sharp cheddar cheese (optional)

2-inch or 1 ½ -inch biscuit cutter

Preheat regular oven to 425° or convection oven to 400°. Lightly grease baking sheet.

Mix flour and sugar. Divide shortening into 4 parts on top of flour mixture and cut into flour until size of large pea. (Two knives will do this, but a dough blender works better.) Mix in cheese (optional). Pour in buttermilk and stir with large spoon until well blended.

Lightly flour board, your hands, and rolling pin. Scoop out half of dough with spoon and gently make a ball using your fingers as much as possible instead of the palms of your hands. Place dough on board and pat one time to make flat place to start rolling pin. Lightly roll dough from center out until about ½-inch thick. The lighter the stroke, the better.

Cut biscuits, dipping cutter into flour each

time. If biscuit sticks on cutter and readily comes off board, the dough is perfect and biscuit can be flipped out onto your hand and quickly placed on baking sheet. Leave ½ inch between biscuits so they do not touch each other or sides of baking sheet. After cutting first half of dough, gently gather scraps together and set aside before starting second half. Cut biscuits from second half of dough. Mix scraps from remaining dough and gently form a ball, mashing with your fingers only enough to hold dough together. Handling too much makes for tough biscuits. Don't flour hands, dough, rolling pin, or cutter when working with these last biscuits. Roll and cut. Bake in either oven 10 minutes, or until lightly browned, and serve immediately.

NOTES: To make biscuits 2 or 3 hours before serving, cut out, place on baking sheet, cover with wax paper, and set in a cool place until ready to bake.

To freeze, bake for 5 minutes, or until biscuits begin to brown. Cool to room temperature and freeze. When ready to bake, place on greased baking sheet, thaw completely, and bake at 425° for 5 minutes, or until hot and lightly browned.

Swedish Cream

Carol Saunders (Mrs. Donald) of Columbia gave us this recipe, and it is the most elegant dessert we serve.

Serves 10

1 cup sugar
1 envelope unflavored gelatin
1 cup heavy whipping cream
1 cup half-and-half
1 teaspoon pure vanilla extract
2 cups sour cream

10 (4-ounce) molds lightly sprayed with
    vegetable spray
2-quart saucepan

Combine sugar and gelatin. Add cream and half-and-half. Heat on medium 5 minutes, stirring constantly, until hot but not boiling. Sugar and gelatin must be completely dissolved. If it gets too hot or cooks too long, it will be tough. Cool 10 minutes. Combine vanilla and sour cream and stir into warm mixture. Ladle into molds. Refrigerate 2 hours, or until set. Unmold Swedish Cream by running a knife around edges and turning out.

Serve with seasonal fruit. In winter, we use fresh oranges in Orange-Brandy Sauce (p.55). In spring and summer, we use raspberries with Raspberry Sauce, strawberries, blackberries, blueberries, or peaches.

Raspberry Sauce

10 servings for Swedish Cream or Chocolate Pie (p.85)

2 pints fresh raspberries
¼ cup fresh lemon juice
½ cup confectioners' sugar
4 teaspoons cornstarch
¼ cup water
¾ cup Chambord® liqueur

Process 1 pint of raspberries until puréed. Add lemon juice. Strain to remove seeds. Process with confectioners' sugar until well mixed. Pour into top of double boiler over, but not touching, simmering water. Dissolve cornstarch in water. Mix well and stir into raspberries. Cook over simmering water 5 minutes, or until sauce thickens and coats a spoon. Add ½ cup Chambord® and cook 2 minutes. Remove from heat and cool.

Toss remaining pint of raspberries in remaining Chambord®. Ladle sauce over each dessert and divide raspberries between each.

Crab Salad in the Dining Room
of the Blacklock House

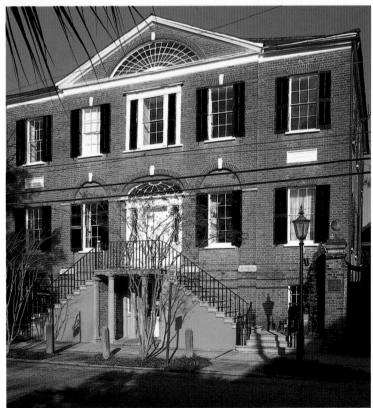

Reception after the
Performance
Sottile Theater

TOASTED PECANS
BOILED CREEK SHRIMP
WITH
MAYONNAISE SAUCE
OPEN-FACED CUCUMBER AND TOMATO SANDWICHES
KIWI, CANTALOUPE, ORANGES, BANANAS
WITH
VANILLA AND CHOCOLATE SAUCES

CHAMPAGNE
MINERAL WATER

Boiled Creek Shrimp

There can be as many as 75 small creek shrimp per pound.

1 quart water
1 teaspoon salt
1 bay leaf
1 pound creek shrimp, unpeeled

Bring salted water and bay leaf to a boil on high. Add shrimp and return to full boil. Shrimp will be pink, curled, and done. This takes only about 3 minutes, so watch carefully. Drain shrimp in colander, spread on baking sheet, and sprinkle lightly and quickly with cold water to stop further cooking. Peel when cool enough to handle.

Mayonnaise Sauce

Tiny creek shrimp are so sweet and delicate that you don't want to overpower them with a strong sauce.

Approximately ¾ cup

⅔ cup Hellmann's® mayonnaise
2 Tablespoons ketchup
1 Tablespoon + 2 teaspoons fresh lemon juice
Pinch salt
Pinch cayenne pepper
½ teaspoon curry powder (optional)

Combine mayonnaise, ketchup, lemon juice, salt, cayenne pepper, and optional curry powder. Refrigerate.

Open-Faced Cucumber Sandwiches

Myrna Barkoot works at the President's House and gave us the recipe for these open-faced sandwiches.

40 party-size rounds

20 slices thin-sliced white bread
½ cup Hellmann's® mayonnaise
½ cup sour cream
4 Tablespoons minced onion
5 Tablespoons chopped fresh parsley
¼ teaspoon salt
½ teaspoon black pepper
1 pound large cucumbers
Salt
White pepper

2½-inch biscuit cutter

Cut 40 rounds from bread. Mix mayonnaise, sour cream, onion, half of parsley, salt, and black pepper. Spread a rounded half-teaspoon of mayonnaise mixture on each round. Peel cucumbers, slice ¼-inch thick, and place on top of mayonnaise. Sprinkle with salt, white pepper, and remaining half of parsley.

Open-Faced Tomato Sandwiches

40 party-size rounds

20 slices thin-sliced white bread
1 cup Hellmann's® mayonnaise
6 Tablespoons chopped fresh basil
½ teaspoon black pepper
1 pound small very ripe tomatoes
Salt
White pepper

2½-inch biscuit cutter

Cut 40 rounds from bread. Mix mayonnaise, 4 Tablespoons basil, and black pepper. Spread a rounded half-teaspoon of mayonnaise mixture on each round. Slice tomatoes ⅓-inch thick and place on top of mayonnaise. Sprinkle with salt, white pepper, and remaining basil.

Chocolate Sauce

This is a perfect chocolate sauce for fruit because it's not so rich and heavy and doesn't overwhelm the flavor of the fruit.

3 cups

1 cup half-and-half
1 cup light corn syrup
2 cups semisweet chocolate chips

Combine half-and-half and corn syrup in saucepan with whisk. Heat on low until hot but not boiling. Add chocolate chips, whisking constantly for 5 minutes, or until chips are melted and mixture has thickened. Serve at room temperature.

Vanilla or Amaretto Fruit Sauce

Never underestimate pure vanilla. The Vanilla Dip is wonderful, but the Amaretto Dip is just as good and makes a nice change.

2 ½ cups

½ cup confectioners' sugar
2 Tablespoons pure vanilla extract or amaretto liqueur
2 cups sour cream

Whisk sugar and vanilla or amaretto until completely blended. Whisk into sour cream. Serve or refrigerate.

Toasted Pecans

1 pound pecan halves
4 Tablespoons butter, melted
Salt

Preheat oven to 350°.

Toss pecans in melted butter, bake at 350° for 15 minutes, and sprinkle with salt. Cool.

Cougar Club Party
Remley's Point

BOILED PEANUTS AND SEASONED OYSTER CRACKERS

LOWCOUNTRY SHRIMP AND CRAB BOIL
WANDO COCKTAIL SAUCE
FRESH CORN ON THE COB
COUNTRY SAUSAGE
MARINATED SWEET SLAW
REMLEY'S POINT CORN BREAD MUFFINS
OR SKILLET CORN BREAD
PEANUT BUTTER AND JELLY SANDWICHES

WATERMELON
LEMON STICKIES

ICED TEA
HOMEMADE LEMONADE
SOFT DRINKS
BOTTLED WATER

Boiled Peanuts

Patrick Duddy, who works for ARAMARK Corporation, has helped plan every detail of many of our parties at the College. This is his recipe for boiled peanuts.

8 to 10 servings

2 quarts green uncooked peanuts in shell
½ cup salt
1 gallon water

3-gallon pot with lid

Wash peanuts in cold water until clean. Bring salted water to a boil. Add peanuts and cover. Reduce heat to low and simmer 2½ to 3 hours, or until nuts inside shells are soft. Open one of the largest to test. Turn off heat, remove lid, and let peanuts soak 1 hour. Drain and serve.

NOTE: Boiled peanuts sour if left unrefrigerated for more than 12 hours.

Seasoned Oyster Crackers

Serves 18 to 20 people as hors d'oeuvre

6 cups oyster crackers (10-ounce package)
1 package Hidden Valley Original Ranch® dressing mix
1 Tablespoon lemon pepper
1 Tablespoon dill weed
1 cup vegetable oil

Shallow baking pan

Preheat oven to 350°.

Spread oyster crackers on a baking pan. Sprinkle with dry dressing mix, lemon pepper, and dill weed. Pour oil over and mix well. Bake at 350° for 12 minutes, or until golden brown. Stir halfway through baking. Remove from baking pan and cool.

Peanut Butter and Jelly Sandwiches

To be certain that everybody has something they like to eat, include these sandwiches on a picnic. To make them even more enticing, cut them with cookie cutters. At the Remley's Point Shrimp and Crab Boil, the Peanut Butter and Jelly Sandwiches were shaped like fish.

8 sandwiches

1 cup smooth peanut butter
¾ cup grape jelly
1 Tablespoon Hellmann's® mayonnaise
1 loaf thin-sliced white bread

Combine peanut butter, jelly, and mayonnaise in food processor or electric mixer. Refrigerate until 30 minutes before making sandwiches.

Marinated Sweet Slaw

Elyce Robinson (Mrs. Ralph C.) of Columbia gave us this recipe when we were cooking at Trinity Cathedral.

Serves 12

2 pounds green cabbage, washed and outer leaves removed
¼ jumbo yellow onion, chopped
1 green pepper, cored, seeded, and chopped
¾ cup vegetable oil
1 cup apple cider vinegar
½ cup sugar
1 Tablespoon salt
1 Tablespoon celery seeds
1 teaspoon dry mustard

Grate cabbage. Combine cabbage, onion, and pepper. Bring oil, vinegar, sugar, salt, celery seeds and dry mustard to a boil and pour over cabbage mixture. Cover and refrigerate overnight. Drain before serving.

Lowcountry Shrimp and Crab Boil

Serves 8

3 gallons water
3 Tablespoons salt
6 bay leaves
1 Tablespoon whole black peppercorns
1 jumbo yellow onion, sliced
1 carrot, sliced in thin rounds
Leaves of 1 stalk celery
16 (2 x 1-inch) links uncooked fresh country
  sausage
2 pounds medium shrimp, unpeeled
8 live crabs
8 ears fresh corn

5-gallon pot
Iron skillet

Lemon quarters
Wando Cocktail Sauce

Combine water, salt, bay leaves, peppercorns, onion, carrot, and celery leaves in pot.

Cover and bring to a boil on high. Reduce to medium and boil 30 to 40 minutes to develop flavors.

Cook sausage in iron skillet with $\frac{1}{4}$-inch of water on medium 20 to 25 minutes, or until sausage is dark brown on outside and cooked through. The inside should be gray with no pink showing.

Bring water back to a hard boil. Add shrimp, crabs, corn, and sausage. Cover, return to a boil, and boil 5 minutes, or until crabs are red, shrimp are curled and pink, corn is tender, and sausage is hot. Dip contents out with large strainer or sieve into bowls or platters and serve with lemon quarters and Wando Cocktail Sauce.

Wando Cocktail Sauce

2 cups ketchup
2 Tablespoons prepared horseradish
2 teaspoons Worcestershire sauce
4 teaspoons fresh lemon juice

Combine ingredients. Refrigerate up to one week. Makes 2 cups.

Remley's Point Corn Bread Muffins or Skillet Corn Bread

Serves 8

¼ cup vegetable oil
½ cup all-purpose flour
1 ½ cups plain yellow corn meal
  (we use Adluh)
1 Tablespoon baking powder
2 teaspoons salt
2 teaspoons sugar
2 eggs
1 ¼ cups milk

Two iron muffin pans for 6 muffins each or one (10-inch) iron skillet

Preheat oven to 425°.

The loaves and the fishes

Divide oil between muffin pans, swish around to grease, and heat oil and pans in oven until smoking hot. Mix flour, corn meal, baking powder, salt, and sugar. Add eggs and milk and mix very lightly by hand until eggs "disappear." However, do not mix until batter is smooth; lumpy batter makes better corn bread. Remove pans from oven and pour the hot oil from pans into batter. Stir batter lightly with spoon, and pour back into sizzling pans. Hot pans are the key. This is a dangerous step. Be very careful not to burn yourself.

Bake muffins at 425° for 10 minutes, or until they begin to brown. (They are so small that if they become golden brown they will be too dry.) If using skillet instead of muffin pans, bake corn bread for 20 minutes, or until lightly browned. Serve immediately.

Corn Bread for 120

When making this corn bread we have always used Adluh self-rising yellow cornmeal, which is made in Columbia.

120 (2 x 2) pieces

1 (1-pound) can Crisco® shortening
1 (5-pound) bag self-rising yellow cornmeal
½ pound self-rising flour
1 Tablespoon salt
6 Tablespoons sugar
12 eggs, lightly beaten
½ gallon milk
½ gallon buttermilk

Two (26 x 18) pans, greased with shortening

Preheat regular oven to 425° or convection oven to 400°.

Melt shortening and cool.

Mix cornmeal, flour, salt, and sugar. Add eggs and mix very lightly by hand until eggs "disappear." Add milk and buttermilk and stir gently. Add melted shortening and gently mix. Do not mix until batter is smooth; lumpy batter makes better corn bread.

Pour batter into greased pans and bake in either oven for 15 minutes, or until it starts to brown and begins to pull away from sides of pans.

Homemade Lemonade

Alex keeps this lemonade in the refrigerator all summer long. Use a little more lemon juice and a little less water for tarter lemonade. Use a little more syrup and a little less water for sweeter lemonade.

Serves 8

SIMPLE SYRUP
1 cup boiling water
2 cups sugar

LEMONADE
1 cup fresh lemon juice
1 cup simple syrup
2 cups small ice cubes or crushed ice
1 quart cold water

TO MAKE SIMPLE SYRUP: Add sugar to boiling water, stirring until dissolved. Cool to room temperature.

TO MAKE LEMONADE: Mix all ingredients together, stirring vigorously. Pour over ice and serve.

Lemon Stickies

These could be described as "mock lemon squares." Carole Clark (Mrs. David) of Columbia gave us this recipe, and it's a favorite for all age groups.

192 bite-size pieces

CRUST
3 boxes high-quality lemon cake mix
3 sticks butter, melted
3 eggs
Juice of 2 lemons

18 x 26 baking sheet, lightly greased

TOPPING
3 (8-ounce) packages cream cheese, room
  temperature
3 boxes confectioners' sugar
6 eggs

Preheat convection oven to 325°.

Combine lemon cake mix, melted butter, eggs, and lemon juice in large institutional mixer and mix well. Pour onto baking sheet.

Beat cream cheese until smooth. Beat in confectioners' sugar and eggs. Spread over crust mixture and bake at 325° for 35 minutes, or until golden brown. Cool. Cut 6 x 12.

The Round Table
Randolph Hall

CORN CHOWDER WITH MELBA TOAST

OVEN-POACHED SALMON WITH SAUTÉED LEEKS
ROASTED NEW POTATOES
SAUTÉED FRESH SPINACH
COLLEGE BISCUITS

LEMON MOUSSE WITH LEMON CURD
SANDIES

ICED TEA
WHITE WINE
COFFEE
CRYSTALLIZED GINGER

Corn Chowder

This is a rich, thick soup recipe from Maybry Limehouse of Columbia. It is hearty enough for a meal or, in a smaller 6-ounce serving, for a first course. A good brand of frozen corn can be substituted for fresh corn, but fresh yellow corn makes a prettier and better chowder.

Serves 8

5 cups fresh corn, cut off cob
5 slices bacon
5 Tablespoons finely chopped jumbo yellow
   onion
2 teaspoons tarragon
2 teaspoons marjoram
4 Tablespoons butter
¼ teaspoon sugar (if corn is not sweet enough
   for your taste)
4 Tablespoons all-purpose flour
3 cups milk
3 cups heavy whipping cream
1 Tablespoon salt
1 teaspoon white pepper

3-gallon pot

Process corn in food processor until fine. Fry bacon until crisp. Reserve fat. Process bacon and reserve. Sauté onion in bacon fat on medium 3 minutes, or until soft. Add tarragon, marjoram, butter, and reserved bacon. Add corn (and sugar, if desired) and cook on medium 15 minutes, or until corn softens. Sprinkle flour over corn, mix well, and cook 5 minutes, stirring occasionally. Stir in milk, cream, salt, and pepper. Cook on low, stirring occasionally, 15 minutes, or until thick. Do not boil.

Corn Chowder for 150

8 pounds bacon
7 jumbo yellow onions, chopped
14 pounds frozen corn
2 Tablespoons sugar (if corn is not sweet enough
   for your taste)
3 Tablespoons tarragon
3 Tablespoons marjoram
3 pounds butter
6 cups all-purpose flour
6 gallons milk
4 Tablespoons salt
4 teaspoons white pepper

Two (18 x 26) baking sheets
Two (5-gallon) pots

Preheat convection oven to 325°.

Divide bacon between baking sheets and pan-fry bacon in convection oven. Remove bacon when brown and reserve. Divide fat equally between the two pots and heat on medium. Divide onions and cook until soft. Divide corn and cook until tender. Add sugar if desired. Divide tarragon, marjoram, and butter between pots. Stir flour into each until there are no flour lumps. Cook 15 minutes, stirring occasionally. Chop cooked bacon and divide between pots. Gradually add milk, salt, and pepper to each and cook on low, stirring occasionally, until thick. Do not boil.

Melba Toast

16 pieces

4 slices thin-sliced white bread
2 Tablespoons butter, melted

Preheat oven to 350°.

Cut crusts off bread and cut into 4 triangles. Brush both sides with butter. Bake at 350° for 15 minutes, or until dry and golden brown.

Oven-Poached Salmon with Sautéed Leeks

Lee Godbey, the ARAMARK Corporation Catering Service Chef at the College of Charleston, prepares this salmon for 500 people, and every fillet is perfect.

Serves 8

8 (6-ounce) skinless salmon fillets
2 teaspoons salt
1 teaspoon white pepper
1 cup white wine
1 stick butter
1 Tablespoon fresh lemon juice
3 Tablespoons chopped fresh dill

White part of 8 leeks, julienned
2 Tablespoons olive oil
1 teaspoon salt

9 x 13 glass baking dish
12-inch frying pan

Preheat oven to 350°.

Salt and pepper fillets on both sides and place in baking dish.

Cook wine, butter, and lemon juice in frying pan on medium, whisking constantly. Whisk constantly 10 minutes, or until reduced by half. Pour over salmon, sprinkle with dill, and cover tightly with aluminum foil. Bake at 350° for 20 minutes, or until no longer translucent when pierced at thickest point.

Fillets can be set aside and reheated for 5 minutes at 350° when ready to serve. Heat 1 Tablespoon olive oil in frying pan. Add half of leeks, sprinkle with $\frac{1}{4}$ teaspoon salt, and sauté 5 minutes, or until leeks are limp and beginning to brown. Remove from pan and sauté remaining leeks in same manner. Using a spatula, place salmon on individual plates or platter and top with leeks.

Roasted New Potatoes

Tarragon or your favorite herb or seasoning can be added for the last 5 minutes of cooking.

Serves 8

1 teaspoon pressed garlic (about 4 large cloves)
1 cup olive oil
3 $\frac{1}{2}$ pounds new potatoes
Salt
Black pepper

Marinate garlic in olive oil overnight.

Preheat oven to 425°.
Brush a baking sheet with some of the garlic olive oil.

Wash unpeeled potatoes and quarter or cut in approximately 1 $\frac{1}{2}$-inch pieces. Put in large bowl, pour remaining garlic olive oil over, toss until coated, and sprinkle with salt and pepper. Place on baking sheet skin side up and not touching.

Roast potatoes at 425° for 15 minutes. Turn to brown the other side. Sprinkle with fresh herbs or seasonings and roast 5 minutes, or until skin is crisp and potatoes are tender when pierced with a fork. Can be set aside at this point. When ready to serve, heat at 350° for 5 minutes, or until hot. Sprinkle with salt and pepper to taste.

Sautéed Fresh Spinach
See page 3

College Biscuits
See page 3

Lemon Mousse with Lemon Curd

This is Marion Sullivan's recipe. *(This recipe contains raw egg whites, which are not acceptable to many cooks.)*

Serves 8

CURD
3 eggs
2 egg yolks
1 cup sugar
¼ cup fresh lemon juice (about 2 lemons)
1 Tablespoon finely chopped lemon zest
1 stick cold butter, cut into 8 pieces

MOUSSE
1 envelope unflavored gelatin
¼ cup cold water
5 eggs, separated
¾ cup fresh lemon juice (about 5 lemons)
2 teaspoons finely chopped lemon zest
1 ½ cups sugar
1 cup heavy whipping cream

TO MAKE CURD: Put eggs and yolks in top of double boiler over, but not touching, simmering water and whisk lightly. Gradually whisk in sugar. Whisk in lemon juice and zest. Cook, whisking constantly, 10 minutes, or until thick. Add cold butter and whisk until mixture thickens again. Cool to room temperature. Curd will keep for 3 days tightly covered in refrigerator or a month in freezer.

TO MAKE MOUSSE: Sprinkle gelatin over water to soften. Whisk egg yolks, lemon juice, lemon zest, and ¾ cup sugar in top of double boiler over, but not touching, simmering water. Whisk constantly, 8 to 10 minutes, or until mixture begins to thicken. Remove from heat, add gelatin to hot mixture, and whisk to dissolve. Chill 45 minutes to 1 hour, or until it mounds slightly.

Once lemon mixture is sufficiently chilled, whip egg whites in electric mixer 3 to 4 minutes, or until they begin to hold their shape. Gradually whip in remaining ¾ cup sugar until egg whites form soft peaks. Whip cream until it forms soft peaks. Fold a fourth of whites into chilled lemon mixture to soften. Fold in remaining whites and whipped cream. Spoon ¾ cup of mousse into 8 wine glasses, layering with 2 rounded Tablespoons of chilled lemon curd. Swirl mousse and curd with a spoon to integrate them, but do not completely mix curd into mousse. It's nice to have a little taste of lemon curd throughout. Refrigerate 1 hour.

Sandies

To make Pecan Sandies, add 1 cup chopped pecans to the dough after adding flour.

5 dozen

2 sticks butter, room temperature
⅓ cup sugar
1 Tablespoon pure vanilla extract
2 cups all-purpose flour
1 cup confectioners' sugar

Preheat oven to 350°.

Cream butter, sugar, and vanilla in electric mixer on medium. Add flour and mix well. Pinch off pieces of dough and roll into balls about the size of a quarter. Place on baking sheets and flatten slightly with hand. Bake at 350° for 12 minutes, or until very lightly browned. Sift confectioners' sugar over cookies immediately. When ready to serve, another thin layer of confectioners' sugar makes them sweeter and prettier. These cookies will keep only 2 days.

CRYSTALLIZED GINGER: This makes a nice ending to a meal. It can usually be found on the gourmet food shelf of grocery stores or in specialty food shops.

Fall Oyster Roast and
Pig Picking
Dixie Plantation

STEAMED OYSTERS

BARBECUED PIG
BARBECUED SHRIMP
COLLEGE OF CHARLESTON QUAIL
BROWN RICE
RED RICE
SLAW
DIXIE PLANTATION YEAST ROLLS

WINTER FRUIT TORTE

ICED TEA
RED AND WHITE WINE

College of Charleston Quail (Game Chicken)

This recipe was my mother's, Margaret Dutrow (Mrs. Ray H., Jr.). Sixteen quail or boneless chicken breasts are more than enough for eight people. This is also good for doves. The recipe can be increased to serve as many people as you would like to serve, but, surprisingly, the one-hour cooking time remains the same.

Serves 8

16 (4 to 5-ounce) quail or boneless chicken
   breasts
12 ounces extra-virgin olive oil
Salt
Pepper
Oregano
4 cups all-purpose flour
1 ½ sticks butter
2 large green peppers, cored, seeded, and chopped
2 jumbo yellow onions, chopped
6 Tablespoons tomato paste
⅓ cup dry sherry
6 cups water
2 teaspoons salt
¾ teaspoon black pepper
2 pounds mushrooms, cleaned and quartered into
   bite-size pieces
1 ½ cups fresh white bread crumbs, torn by hand
   as finely as possible

12-inch frying pan
Roasting pan or 2 (4-quart) baking dishes

Preheat oven to 350°.

Toss quail in olive oil. Sprinkle generously with salt, pepper, and oregano. Roll in flour. Reserve leftover oil and seasonings. Heat butter in frying pan on medium high until hot but not smoking. Sauté quail until brown all over. Place birds close together, breast side up, in roasting pan. Add reserved olive oil and seasonings to drippings in frying pan and heat on medium high. Add green peppers and onions and sauté 10 to 15 minutes, or until peppers are soft and onions clear. Whisk together tomato paste, sherry, water, salt, and pepper. Pour over peppers and onions, cover, and simmer on low 10 minutes, or until mixture begins to thicken. Add mushrooms and bread crumbs, mix well, and pour over quail. Cover and bake quail at 350° for 1 hour. Set aside at least 1 hour before serving. Spoon gravy over quail and reheat 15 minutes, or until hot. Serve quail on a platter and sauce in a gravy boat.

NOTE: For some reason, this gravy is too thin when it comes out of the oven. After an hour it generally thickens up. But if it's still too thin, thicken with an extra cup of bread crumbs. Add salt and pepper to taste after adding extra bread crumbs. Freezes well.

Barbecued Shrimp

The first time we used this marinade was for the October party at Dixie Plantation. Lee Godbey, who is a genius, changed my Fruit Salad Dressing recipe slightly and used it for the marinade. We've been using it ever since.

Enough for 3 pounds of shrimp

¼ cup fresh lemon juice
¼ cup apple cider vinegar
2 Tablespoons minced onion
¼ cup sugar
2 teaspoons paprika
1 teaspoon dry mustard
1 teaspoon salt
1 teaspoon black pepper
1 cup extra-virgin olive oil
3 pounds medium shrimp, peeled and deveined
   but with tails left on

Long thin wooden skewers, soaked in water until ready to use

In blender or food processor, purée lemon juice, vinegar, onion, sugar, paprika, mustard, salt, and pepper and slowly add olive oil in a thin stream. Pour marinade over raw shrimp. Cover and refrigerate 1 hour. Grill 3 shrimp to a skewer on a hot grill for 3 to 6 minutes on each side, or until shrimp are pink and firm. Cooking time depends on size of shrimp.

Slaw

This is the recipe for the slaw served at Lilfred's in Rembert, S.C. John Kelly, who now lives in Charleston and works at Slightly North of Broad, gave us the recipe.

Serves 8

2 pounds green cabbage,
  washed and outer leaves removed
1 large green pepper, cored and seeded
2 Tablespoons jumbo yellow onion,
  or to taste
2 cups Hellmann's® mayonnaise
1 teaspoon salt
1 1/4 teaspoons finely ground black
  pepper
Sugar (optional)

Slaw for 180

1 (50-pound) bag green cabbage,
  washed and outer leaves removed
30 green peppers, cored and seeded
3 jumbo yellow onions, or to taste
1 1/2 gallons Hellmann's® mayonnaise
6 Tablespoons salt, or to taste
8 Tablespoons finely ground black
  pepper, or to taste
Sugar (optional)

Chop cabbage in food processor until fine. Purée green pepper in food processor. Reserve juice. Grate onion on hand grater until you have 2 Tablespoons of grated onion plus juice. Mix green pepper and its juice with onion and its juice and toss with cabbage. Add mayon-

naise, salt, and pepper and mix well.

Tightly cover slaw and refrigerate overnight. Liquid should be drained off before serving. Serve very cold with slotted spoon.

Dixie Plantation Yeast Rolls

Alex makes this modified version of the recipe from the Parker House Hotel in Boston. Some practice is required to develop the proper "touch."

16 rolls

1 package active dry yeast
1/4 cup warm water (110º)
1 cup scalded milk
1/4 cup sugar
1/4 cup shortening
1 Tablespoon salt
3 1/2-4 cups all-purpose Adluh flour
1 egg
2 Tablespoons butter, melted

Baking sheet

Dissolve yeast in warm water. Combine scalded milk, sugar, shortening, and salt. Cool to lukewarm. Add 1 cup flour. Beat well. Beat in softened yeast and egg. Gradually add remaining flour to form soft dough ball, beating well. Knead for 5 minutes. Cover in bowl and let rise in warm place (85-95º) until doubled in size (1 1/2-2 hours). Turn onto floured board. Shape into balls 2 1/2 inches in diameter. Make crease in each ball with the back of a knife. Brush with melted butter and fold over. Let rise again until doubled (1-1 1/4 hours). Bake at 400º for 15 minutes.

Winter Fruit Torte

8 servings

2 eggs
1 ½ cups sugar
1 teaspoon pure vanilla extract
4 Tablespoons all-purpose flour
2 ½ teaspoons baking powder
¼ teaspoon salt
1 ½ cups peeled and chopped Granny Smith
*   apples*
1 ½ cups peeled and chopped firm pears
1 cup fresh cranberries
1 cup chopped pecans

Soft Whipped Cream (p.58)
1 Granny Smith apple and 1 Red Delicious
    apple for garnish

11 x 7 x 2 (1 ½ -quart) rectangular baking
    pan or Pyrex® dish, greased

Preheat oven to 325°.

Beat eggs in electric mixer until light in color. Gradually beat in sugar and continue to beat until eggs are light and fluffy. Beat in vanilla. Mix flour, baking powder, and salt and fold into egg mixture. Add apples, pears, cranberries, and pecans and mix well. Pour into pan and bake at 325° for 45 minutes, or until top has a brown crust. Serve warm with Soft Whipped Cream and 1 slice of each apple.

Brown Rice

Serves 8

2 cups Uncle Ben's Converted® Brown Rice
1 ⅛ teaspoons salt
4 cups chicken broth, fresh or canned
2 Tablespoons butter
1 cup chopped onion
1 pound medium-size mushrooms, cleaned and
*   quartered (optional)*

½ teaspoon white pepper

3-quart heavy saucepan with lid
12-inch frying pan

Combine rice, 1 teaspoon salt, and chicken broth in saucepan. Stir and bring to boil on high. Cover, reduce to low, and simmer 30 to 35 minutes, or until all liquid is absorbed. A spoon slipped down the side to the bottom should come up with almost dry, shiny rice. Place in bowl and cover lightly with aluminum foil. The rice can be held at this point until ready to serve.

When ready to serve, heat butter in frying pan until hot but not smoking. Add onions, mushrooms (optional), the remaining ⅛ teaspoon salt and pepper, and mix well. Turn heat to medium and sauté onions (and mushrooms) for 5 minutes, or until onions are clear (and mushrooms begin to brown). Add rice and toss until hot.

Steamed Oysters
See page 137

Barbecued Pig
See page 30

Red Rice
See page 142

Oyster Roast and Pig Picking at Dixie Plantation

Parents Weekend
The Cistern

BARBECUED PIG
RICE
OR
COLLEGE "MYSTERY MEAT"
WITH
MASHED POTATOES

BUTTER BEANS
CORN ON THE COB
MARINATED SWEET SLAW

HOMEMADE LEMONADE
ICED TEA

PERSIMMON CAKE
APPLE CRISP

Barbecued Pig

Jim Quinn is an advisor for Pi Kappa Phi at the College of Charleston, where the national fraternity was founded in 1904. He is also a lawyer for the S.C. Department of Natural Resources, but he is famous all over the state for his barbecue. This is his recipe in his own words.

Serves 60 with 95-100 pound pig or 75 with 125 pound pig, using the same recipe

PIG
95-100 pound or 125 pound pig
Salt and Pepper

SAUCE
2 gallons apple cider vinegar
¾ cup coarse black pepper
¾ cup crushed red pepper flakes
1 (1-pound) box salt
1 cup TEXAS PETE® Hot Sauce

Mix all ingredients together.

Butterfly pig (backbone is split but pig is not completely cut in half). Salt and pepper pig liberally. Prepare bed of 20-25 pounds charcoal in a pit or metal cooker. Use Kingsford™ charcoal. Hickory coals may be used instead of charcoal, or hickory chips may be sprinkled over charcoal. Plan to use about 140 pounds charcoal for a pit and 100 pounds for a cooker. When charcoal is burning evenly, spread out and place the pig bone side down on grate over coals. Cover pit with cardboard or shut cooker. After about 1 hour, light 10-15 pounds charcoal on side. Keep this side fire going and use periodically to stoke the pit or cooker. Maintain grate temperature at 225-240° (just hot enough to keep grease dripping). Turn pig skin side down after about 11 hours on pit or 8 hours in cooker. Pits will cook a pig in about 12 hours. Most cookers will take about 9 hours. The pig is done when meat pulls away from bones and shreds easily. Shred meat,

remove large bones, and return meat to skin for basting. Baste liberally with sauce every 20 minutes for approximately the last hour, cooking the sauce into the meat.

Pig is self-served from the skin ("pig picking"). Extra sauce is served on the side. The sauce is a HOT BBQ sauce. Some of the pepper and TEXAS PETE® can be reduced for the faint of heart. There are a variety of good commercial grade mustard sauces (or mix hot dog mustard, vinegar, and pepper to desired consistency). Use about 1 gallon for the pig. Ketchup-based sauces are outlandish creations usually concocted by persons from other parts of the country.

College of Charleston "Mystery Meat"

This recipe will turn a truly disgusting piece of meat—one that looks like a random animal which has been hit by a truck, i.e., a "road kill"—into something really grand. The pineapple juice will tenderize a MICHELIN® radial. The recipe is entirely suitable for all kinds of meat. (This is Alex's recipe.)

Serves 8

5-6 pound slab of meat from an indefinite
  origin (venison, elk, moose, buffalo, or,
  if you insist, beef chuck roast)
3 large (46-ounce) cans pineapple juice
3 pounds beef suet or pork fat
  (substitute, if you must, 1 pound bacon)
4 Tablespoons salt
4 Tablespoons black pepper
12 large Wadmalaw Sweet Onions cut into
  half-rings (may substitute Vidalias)
4 Tablespoons + 1 teaspoon hot dog mustard
  (no substitutes)
1 Tablespoon Kitchen Bouquet®
3 cups all-purpose flour
½ cup red wine
12 cups beef bouillon
4 dashes Worcestershire sauce

1 bay leaf
Chopped parsley

Large iron skillet or frying pan
Iron Dutch oven

Wrap meat in clean bath towel, put in large pan, pour pineapple juice over, refrigerate and marinate 6 hours. Melt fat in iron skillet or frying pan. Remove cracklings. Sprinkle 1 Tablespoon salt and 1 Tablespoon pepper over onions. Sauté onions in fat until soft. Remove onions. Add 4 Tablespoons mustard to onions to make a paste. Add Kitchen Bouquet®. Sprinkle 3 Tablespoons salt and 3 Tablespoons pepper on meat. Cover with flour on both sides and pound vigorously with rolling pin. Brown meat on both sides in remaining fat (you may have to add vegetable oil). Transfer meat to Dutch oven. Deglaze frying pan with wine. Pour frying pan liquid over browned meat. Spread onion mixture on top of meat. Pour in 6 cups bouillon, Worcestershire sauce, and bay leaf. Make sure bouillon mixture is under the meat as well as around it. Simmer on the lowest possible heat that will keep pan barely bubbling until tender (approximately 3-4 hours). Add bouillon as necessary to keep sufficient liquid in pan. Bouillon mixture will automatically become the gravy.

Put one teaspoon of mustard and chopped parsley on top for color.

Mashed Potatoes

Serves 8

6 large baking potatoes (about 3 ½ pounds)
3 cups water
2 teaspoons salt

½ stick butter, melted
½ cup milk
½ cup heavy whipping cream
2 teaspoons salt, or to taste
¼ teaspoon pepper, or to taste

½ cup grated extra sharp cheddar cheese
  (optional)

2-quart baking dish

Peel potatoes and cut in quarters. Place in saucepan with salted water, adding more water to cover if necessary. Bring to boil on high, cover, and boil 30 minutes, or until tender when pierced with a fork. Drain.

Scald milk and cream on medium until hot but not boiling. Mash potatoes in the bowl of an electric mixer by hand with a potato masher. Beat in butter, milk, cream, salt, and pepper until smooth and creamy. Transfer to baking dish. Can be set aside 3 to 4 hours. Grated cheddar cheese can be sprinkled over top if desired. Bake uncovered at 350° for 30 to 45 minutes, or until hot.

NOTE: Some potatoes have more water in them than others and may not need as much milk. They should be creamy, not runny.

Rice

Half a cup of rice is not much, but these amounts can be increased to serve the multitudes. It's so easy, and it's never gummy—every grain of rice stands alone! Pauline Wheat, of Wheat's Sandwich and Catering in Columbia, taught us this trick at Trenholm Road United Methodist Church.

8 (½-cup) servings

1 cup Uncle Ben's Converted® White Rice
1 teaspoon salt
2 cups water

1 ½-quart heavy saucepan with lid

Combine rice, salt, and water in saucepan. Stir, cover, and bring to a boil on high. Reduce to very low and simmer, covered, 25 to 30 minutes, or until liquid is absorbed. A spoon slipped down the side to the bottom should come up with almost dry, shiny rice. Remove from saucepan immediately or rice will overcook.

Place rice in a serving bowl and cover with aluminum foil. The rice will keep for an hour or so before serving.

½ cup raw rice makes 2 cups cooked
1 cup raw rice makes 4 cups cooked
2 cups raw rice make 8 cups cooked
4 cups raw rice make 16 cups cooked

Parents Weekend Persimmon Cake

Barbara Stine (Mrs. Gordon) is the wife of a member of the College's Board of Trustees. The Stines have a persimmon tree in their yard, keep us supplied with persimmons during the season, and taught us how to make this cake.

Serves 24 slices

1 Tablespoon butter, room temperature
Flour for flouring pan
Bundt pan

4 very ripe persimmons
1 ½ teaspoons baking soda
1 stick butter, room temperature
1 ¾ cups sugar
3 eggs
2 teaspoons pure vanilla extract
2 cups all-purpose flour
½ teaspoon salt
1 teaspoon cinnamon
½ teaspoon allspice
¼ teaspoon ground cloves
¾ cup chopped walnuts, toasted
1 Tablespoon finely chopped orange zest
¾ cup currants
Confectioners' sugar

Preheat oven to 350°. Grease and flour pan using the Tablespoon of butter.

Peel persimmons and press pulp through a coarse sieve making a purée. Measure 1 ⅓ cups of purée. Mix baking soda into purée and set aside. Cream butter and sugar in electric mixer on medium until light and fluffy. Add eggs one at a time, beating well after each. Beat in vanilla.

Combine and sift flour, salt, cinnamon, allspice, and cloves. Add to butter mixture and mix well. Mix in persimmon purée, nuts, orange zest, and currants. Pour into pan. Bake at 350° for 50 to 55 minutes, or until cake tester comes out clean. Cool 10 minutes. Turn out onto rack and cool completely. Sprinkle with confectioners' sugar.

Apple Crisp for 150

This is an easy substitute for apple pie. Amelia Siokos (Mrs. Z. John) of Columbia gave us this recipe when we were cooking at Trinity Cathedral.

5 (#10) cans apple pie filling
3 Tablespoons cinnamon
10 cups light brown sugar
7 ½ cups all-purpose flour
7 ½ cups oatmeal
2 pounds + 2 sticks butter

Five (11 ½ x 19 x 2 ½) pans

Preheat convection oven to 350°.

Mix apple pie filling and cinnamon. Divide between pans. Combine sugar, flour, and oatmeal. Cut butter in with pastry blender or 2 knives. Spread mixture equally over pie filling.

Bake at 350° for 1 hour, or until hot and bubbly and top is brown.

Butter Beans
See page 121

Marinated Sweet Slaw
See page 12

Equestrian Team Brunch
Storybook Farm

COUNTRY HAM
FRESH PINEAPPLE WITH FRUIT SALAD DRESSING
SUMMER TOMATO PIE
OR
WINTER TOMATO PIE
FRIED OKRA
COLLEGE CHEESE BISCUITS

EQUESTRIAN TEAM APPLE SPICE CAKE
MUSCADINES AND SCUPPERNONGS

ICED TEA AND ICED COFFEE

Country Ham

We like to serve thinly sliced country ham in 1½-inch party biscuits or 2-inch biscuits (p.3). Spread with Dijonnaise™.

1 (10-12 pound) cured country ham
1 liter bottle ginger ale
1 bottle red wine
6 oranges, quartered
1 (12-ounce) jar molasses
2 Tablespoons whole cloves
1 cup light brown sugar
½ cup Dijon mustard

5-gallon pot
Roasting pan

Most country hams have harmless mold on them and need to be scrubbed with a brush under cold running water. Place ham in pot and cover with cold water, soak for 12 hours, change water, and soak for an additional 12 hours. Empty pot.

Put ginger ale, wine, oranges, and molasses in pot. Stir to mix. Rinse ham with cold water and put back in pot. Add fresh water to cover ham. Bring to a boil, reduce heat, and simmer on low 25 minutes per pound, about 4 hours, or until big bone is loose.

Preheat oven to 350°. Line roasting pan with aluminum foil.

Place ham in pan. With a sharp knife, slice off skin and all but ¼-inch of fat. Score remaining fat with knife, making a diamond pattern on top and sides. Stick cloves in corners of diamonds. Mix brown sugar and mustard and spread over top and sides. Bake at 350° for 30 minutes, or until mustard and brown sugar glaze is shiny, brown, and set.

TO CARVE: The key to carving country ham is having the right knife. The traditional knife is long, thin, and sharp; it will cut paper-thin slices. Cut straight down to the bone near hock. Begin carving slanted slices toward that cut. You'll have only slivers at first, but will get nice, thin slices as you move toward the meaty part of ham.

Fruit Salad Dressing

This recipe is from Eleanor McCullough (Mrs. C. Fred), Alex's aunt in Greenville. We use it with great success on fruit salads. Lee Godbey, our chef, changed it ever so slightly to make the Barbecued Shrimp Marinade.

2 cups

½ cup apple cider vinegar
1 Tablespoon minced jumbo yellow onion
¼ cup sugar
½ teaspoon salt
½ teaspoon black pepper
1 teaspoon paprika
½ teaspoon dry mustard
½ teaspoon curry powder
1 cup vegetable oil
1 teaspoon poppy seeds

Combine vinegar, onion, sugar, salt, pepper, paprika, dry mustard, and curry powder in blender. Slowly add oil in thin stream. Add in poppy seeds. Refrigerate overnight to let flavors meld. Dressing will keep refrigerated for several days. Shake well before serving.

NOTE: This dressing is especially good with cut-up fresh pineapple. Use ½ cup pineapple per person. Toss with dressing and serve on lettuce. It's also excellent with avocado and grapefruit arranged in a pinwheel design on lettuce.

Summer Tomato Pie

Serves 8

2 prebaked 9-inch Easy Pie Crusts

1½ pounds ripe tomatoes
½ teaspoon salt

1 teaspoon black pepper
6 Tablespoons chopped fresh basil
   or 2 Tablespoons dried
1 cup chopped jumbo yellow onion
3 cups (12 ounces) grated extra sharp cheddar
   cheese
1 cup Hellmann's® mayonnaise

Preheat oven to 350°.

Dip tomatoes in boiling water for 1 minute and peel. Slice ½-inch thick. Drain dry on paper towels.

Divide ingredients evenly between the two pies as follows: Cover bottom of crusts with tomatoes. Sprinkle with salt, pepper, and basil. Sprinkle onions on top. Combine cheese and mayonnaise. Cover pies loosely, but completely, spreading mayonnaise mixture with fingers. Do not press this mixture down. When baked, the light and fluffy mayonnaise and cheese mixture will be similar in texture to a quiche.

Bake pies at 350° for 30 to 35 minutes, or until cheese is bubbly and beginning to brown. Remove from oven and let set 20 to 30 minutes before slicing.

Winter Tomato Pie

There are several winter months when tomatoes have very poor texture and no taste. Canned tomatoes are inexpensive and make a good pie. We use dried basil.

Serves 8

2 prebaked 9-inch Easy Pie Crusts

2 (28-ounce) cans whole tomatoes,
   drained, chopped, and juice pressed out
½ teaspoon salt
1 teaspoon black pepper
2 Tablespoons dried basil
1 cup chopped jumbo yellow onion
1 cup Hellmann's® mayonnaise

3 cups (12 ounces) grated extra sharp
   cheddar cheese

Serves 80
20 prebaked institutional 9-inch pie crusts

12 (#10) cans whole tomatoes, drained,
   chopped, and juice pressed out
1 ½ Tablespoons salt
3 Tablespoons + 1 teaspoon black pepper
20 Tablespoons dried basil
5 jumbo yellow onions, chopped
7 ½ pounds grated extra sharp cheddar cheese
10 cups Hellmann's® mayonnaise

Instructions for making Winter Tomato Pie are the same as those for Summer Tomato Pie, except large recipe is baked at 325° in convection oven.

Easy Pie Crust

Sarah Quackenbush (Mrs. James, Sr.) of Columbia taught all of us at Trenholm Road United Methodist Church to make this easy pie crust.

2 (9-inch or 10-inch) bottom crusts or 1 top
   and bottom crust

3 cups all-purpose flour
1 teaspoon salt
1 Tablespoon sugar
1 cup vegetable shortening
6 Tablespoons ice water
1 Tablespoon vinegar
1 egg, lightly beaten

1 ½ teaspoons sugar for top crust of sweet pies

Preheat oven to 400°.

Mix flour, salt, and sugar. Add shortening, cutting in with a pastry blender until mixture resembles coarse meal.

Mix ice water, vinegar, and ½ of the egg.

Stir into flour mixture with a spoon until mixture comes together to form dough. Divide in half.

Form a round disk with each half of dough. Place on lightly floured board and roll ⅛-inch thick. Roll from center out rather than back and forth. Pie crust needs to be 1 inch larger around than pie pan.

Place dough in pie pan and press sides and bottom down with fingertips until all bubbles are pressed out. Prick sides and bottoms with fork. Press dough around rim with the tines of fork or flute with fingertips. Cut off extra dough with a knife or scissors. Brush sides and bottom with remaining egg.

Bake at 400° for 10 minutes, or until light brown.

If top crust is not needed, shape a second crust in pie pan and freeze unbaked. When ready to use, bake still frozen. Will take about 3 more minutes to bake.

If pie needs a top crust, follow instructions for bottom crust but do not prick with fork. Brush with beaten egg. Roll other half of dough out just as you rolled first half and place over pie filling or cut dough in strips and weave across top of filling like a lattice. Lap it over bottom pie crust at least 1 inch around and press edges of top and bottom together with a fork or crimp with fingers. This will seal top and bottom crusts and hold in juices. Cut slits in top with a sharp knife to release steam. Brush crust evenly with remaining beaten egg (and sprinkle with sugar).

Fried Okra

For a nice combination, put a little bowl of cherry tomatoes sprinkled with sea salt in the center of a tray of fried okra.

4 cups as hors d'oeuvre

½ cup all-purpose flour
½ cup yellow cornmeal
½ teaspoon salt
4 cups fresh okra, washed and sliced ¼-inch thick*
2 cups vegetable oil
Salt to taste

Iron skillet

Mix flour, cornmeal, and ½ teaspoon salt. Toss damp okra in mixture until each piece is well coated. Heat oil in skillet until hot but not smoking. Fry okra one layer deep on high 5 minutes, or until brown. Reduce heat to medium high if oil starts to burn. Drain on paper towels (changing the towels until they are no longer greasy), and salt to taste.

To reheat and crisp okra, place on baking sheet and heat at 400° for 5 minutes.

* To cook okra as a vegetable dish for lunch or supper, cut okra into ½-inch slices. Cook 1 layer at a time on medium high 15 minutes, or until brown. Drain well.

Equestrian Team Apple Spice Cake

This cake comes from Doris Plott in apple country, Canton, N.C. It's easy to make and actually tastes better the day after it's made.

Serves 16 slices

CAKE
1 Tablespoon butter, room temperature
Flour for flouring pan
Tube pan

1 cup vegetable oil
2 cups sugar
3 eggs
2 teaspoons pure vanilla extract
3 cups all-purpose flour, sifted before measuring
1 teaspoon baking soda
1 teaspoon salt
1 teaspoon cinnamon

1 teaspoon nutmeg
½ teaspoon ground cloves
3 cups peeled and finely diced Golden Delicious apples (about 1 pound or 4 large)
1 ½ cups chopped pecans, toasted

GLAZE
½ cup sugar
¼ cup buttermilk
1 Tablespoon butter
¼ teaspoon baking soda
2 teaspoons pure vanilla extract

TO MAKE CAKE: Preheat oven to 350º. Grease and flour tube pan using the Tablespoon of butter.

Beat oil and sugar in electric mixer on medium for 3 minutes. Add eggs one at a time, beating well after each. Add vanilla and beat well. Combine flour, baking soda, salt, cinnamon, nutmeg, and cloves and mix well. Add dry ingredients to oil and sugar mixture one third at a time, continuing to beat on medium. Stir in apples and pecans by hand. Pour batter into pan and bake at 350º for about 1 hour, or until cake is brown and pulling away from sides of pan. A cake tester should come out clean.

TO MAKE GLAZE: Make glaze while cake is baking. Combine sugar, buttermilk, butter, baking soda, and vanilla in saucepan and boil on medium, stirring occasionally, 4 to 5 minutes, or until slightly thickened. Keep hot until cake is done.

Punch holes in cake with a skewer and pour hot glaze over top. Let cake set in pan 1 hour. Turn out onto cake plate with glazed side up. Cool completely before serving.

College Cheese Biscuits
See College Biscuits page 3

Summer Tomato Pie

Board of Trustees Lunch
The President's
Board Room
Randolph Hall

PRIZEWINNING QUAIL STEW
BROWN RICE
POLE BEANS
SUNRISE GRAPEFRUIT SALAD
COLLEGE CHEESE BISCUITS

PECAN PIE
WITH
SOFT WHIPPED CREAM

ICED TEA
COFFEE

Prizewinning Quail Stew

Alex won first place in the Southeastern Wildlife Game Cooking Contest with this recipe.

The ingredients and the procedure are the same as those in the recipe for the College of Charleston Quail (p.24), except the quail are cooked 15-20 minutes longer, or until the meat is about to fall off the bone. Remove quail from gravy and debone when cool enough to handle. Stir meat into gravy. Can be refrigerated at this point. When ready to serve, reheat at 350° for 15 to 20 minutes, or until hot. Serve over white, brown, or wild rice.

Sunrise Grapefruit Salad

Ruby Lee Hartin (Mrs. Rhett) of Columbia was our neighbor when we were first married. This is one of her recipes and it's an all-time favorite for holidays. It's just as good made in a pan, but not as pretty.

Serves 12

$\frac{1}{4}$ grapefruit each

3 pink grapefruit (large and thick-skinned)
8 ounces cream cheese
4 cups water
4 (3-ounce) packages lemon Jell-O®
$\frac{1}{2}$ cup milk
$\frac{1}{2}$ cup Hellmann's® mayonnaise

1 head leaf lettuce, washed and dried

1 sharp paring knife
1 sharp pair scissors

Serves 32

8 pink grapefruit (large and thick-skinned)
12 ounces cream cheese
7$\frac{1}{2}$ cups water
8 (3-ounce) packages lemon Jell-O®
$\frac{3}{4}$ cup milk
$\frac{3}{4}$ cup Hellmann's® mayonnaise

11$\frac{1}{2}$ x 19 x 2$\frac{1}{2}$ pan

Wash grapefruit and cut in halves. Remove fruit and tough membrane section, being careful not to pierce grapefruit shell or to pull center stem out, leaving a hole. Cut membrane away from center with scissors. Squeeze juice from membrane and shell. A total of 4 cups of fruit and juice (or 7$\frac{1}{2}$ cups for large recipe) is needed.

Cream the cheese in food processor.

Boil water and stir in Jell-O® until dissolved. Pour 1 cup hot Jell-O® (or 1$\frac{1}{2}$ cups hot Jell-O® for large recipe) into cream cheese and process until cheese is softened. Whisk milk and mayonnaise together and pour into cheese mixture. Process until smooth. Leave at room temperature until ready to pour over bottom layer.

Mix remaining Jell-O® with grapefruit and juice. Set halved grapefruit shells in a pan so that they stay level. Pour half of grapefruit and Jell-O® mixture into shells or pan. Refrigerate 2 hours, or until congealed.

Process cream cheese mixture again. Pour over congealed bottom layer in shells or pan, leaving room for last layer of grapefruit and Jell-O® mixture. Refrigerate 30 minutes, or until congealed.

Stir grapefruit and Jell-O® mixture if it has congealed. Fill shells or pan with remaining mixture. Refrigerate 4 hours, or until all is set.

When ready to serve, cut grapefruit shells in half and place on a plate of lettuce. Each serving will be a quarter of a whole grapefruit.

The instructions for making the large recipe for Sunrise Grapefruit Salad are the same as those for the small recipe except that it is congealed in 11 x 19 x 2$\frac{1}{2}$ pan and cut 4 x 8.

NOTES: If put in a pan and tightly covered with plastic wrap before cutting in half, filled grapefruit halves will keep for 4 to 5 days in refrigerator.

Unfortunately, you cannot always find grapefruit that are large and thick-skinned. If only small, thin-skinned grapefruit are available, you will have to use more than we have indicated. In either case, the important thing is to get 4 cups (or 7 ½ cups for large recipe) of combined fruit and juice.

Pole Beans

Pole beans are long, flat beans. Unlike string beans that we have today, the pole beans that I have encountered have strings. I call them "Country Green Beans."

Serves 8

2 pounds pole beans
1 quart water
2 teaspoons salt
Pinch baking soda
¼ teaspoon black pepper
4 Tablespoons bacon fat

3-quart saucepan

Snap ends off beans, pull strings off both sides, and snap in half. Combine beans with water, salt, baking soda, pepper, and bacon fat. Bring to a boil on high, reduce to medium, and place a piece of aluminum foil lightly on top of beans to preserve color. Cook 15 to 20 minutes, depending on tenderness of beans.

Pecan Pie
See page 146

Brown Rice
See page 26

College Cheese Biscuits
See College Biscuits page 3

Alumni Dinner
Simons Center for
Historic Preservation

ONION SOUP WITH CROUTONS
PRESERVATION SALAD

BEEF FILETS
WITH
BÉARNAISE SAUCE
TWICE-BAKED STAND-UP POTATOES
SAUTÉED MUSHROOMS
BROCCOLI
FRENCH BREAD

CREAM CHEESE PIE

ICED TEA
RED WINE
COFFEE

Onion Soup with Croutons

This is a rich soup, thick with onions. It can be multiplied for as many servings as needed.

Serves 8

SOUP
3 Tablespoons butter
1 Tablespoon olive oil
24 cups peeled, thinly sliced jumbo yellow
  onions (about 6 pounds)
1 ½ teaspoons sugar
3 Tablespoons all-purpose flour
1 Tablespoon salt
3 quarts chicken broth, fresh or canned, with
  fat skimmed off
2 cups white wine
1 teaspoon Kitchen Bouquet® (optional)

3-gallon pot

CROUTONS
1 loaf French bread
1 stick butter, melted
1 cup (4 ounces) grated fresh Parmesan or
  Swiss cheese

TO MAKE THE SOUP: Heat butter and olive oil in pot, add onions, cover, and cook on medium, stirring occasionally, 30 minutes, or until onions are soft. Add sugar and cook onions and sugar uncovered 15 minutes, or until sugar browns on bottom of pot. Sugar will look dark brown and almost burned, but it won't taste burned; the browned sugar gives soup a rich brown color. Stir in flour and cook, stirring constantly, 5 minutes, or until there are no lumps. Bring broth to a boil. Stir 2 ladles of broth into onions and mix well, being careful not to have flour lumps. Stir in remaining broth, wine, and salt. Add Kitchen Bouquet® for a darker color. Reduce heat to low and simmer, partially covered, 1 hour. Skim fat off top.
    TO MAKE CROUTONS: Preheat oven to 325°.

Slice French bread into 16 one-inch slices. Brush with melted butter and bake at 325° for 20 minutes, or until golden brown. Sprinkle each crouton with 2 Tablespoons cheese. Broil 30 seconds, or until cheese is melted and beginning to brown. Watch closely; can burn quickly. Place one hot crouton in each bowl. Ladle soup over crouton, place second crouton on side, and serve. Freezes well.

Preservation Salad

Francis Avinger (Mrs. Robert L., Sr.) of Columbia served this salad forty years ago. It's been a favorite in our house, at Trenholm Road, at Trinity, and at the College. A commercial Italian dressing makes a quick and easy substitute for the Garlic Vinaigrette, but I don't recommend any other changes. Boiled shrimp (Fast Method for Boiling Shrimp, p.135) marinated in the dressing and served on top of the salad makes a nice first course.

Serves 8

1 ½ to 2 heads Romaine (a generous handful
  per person), washed, dried, and torn into
  approximately 2-inch long pieces
6 Tablespoons finely grated Parmesan cheese
6 Tablespoons browned benne seeds (p.54)
1 recipe Garlic Vinaigrette Salad Dressing
Parmesan curls for garnish (optional)

GARLIC VINAIGRETTE SALAD DRESSING

1 ⅓ cups

1 cup extra-virgin olive oil
⅓ cup white balsamic vinegar
1 Tablespoon fresh lemon juice
½ to 1 teaspoon pressed fresh garlic
  (1 to 2 cloves)
½ teaspoon salt
¼ teaspoon black pepper
⅛ teaspoon sugar

Combine ingredients in a jar and shake well. Refrigerate overnight to let flavors meld. Dressing will keep refrigerated for several days. Shake well before serving.

TO ASSEMBLE: Combine lettuce, grated Parmesan, and benne seeds and toss. Add dressing and toss. Divide between 8 salad plates and top with Parmesan curls.

Beef Filets

At the Bishop Robert Smith House we don't have a convenient place to use or store a grill, so after 28 years of backyard grilling in Columbia we had to adjust our method of cooking steaks and other grilled food. Much to our surprise, the results are just as good and a lot less trouble.

Serves 8

8 (8-ounce) 1 ½-inch thick beef filets
Salt, black pepper, and garlic powder to taste
1 teaspoon butter
1 teaspoon olive oil

2 large, well-seasoned iron skillets

Sprinkle both sides of filets with salt, pepper, and garlic powder. Plump filets by rounding them up with your hands.

Put ½ teaspoon of butter and ½ teaspoon of olive oil in each skillet. Heat on high until hot but not smoking. Place 4 filets in each skillet and cook 4 minutes, or until bottom sides are blackened.

Turn filets over and cook on other side 2 minutes, or until brown. Reduce heat to medium low. Move filets to sides of skillets and cook on each side for 3 minutes for rare, or 5 minutes for medium. (The center of the skillet is too hot.) One side of the filets should be brown and pretty, but not blackened.

Béarnaise Sauce

Serves 8 with Filets

2 egg yolks, lightly beaten
2 teaspoons white wine vinegar
1 teaspoon dried tarragon
1 teaspoon minced shallots
1 Tablespoon chopped parsley
¼ teaspoon coarsely ground pepper
1 stick cold butter

Follow instructions for Hollandaise Sauce. (p.94)

Twice-Baked Stand-Up Potatoes

This is Alex's recipe, but he thinks that these potatoes may be more trouble than they're worth. We don't agree.

Serves 8

8 baking potatoes
3 Tablespoons butter
2 teaspoons salt
1 teaspoon black pepper
Buttermilk
1 Tablespoon vegetable oil

Bake potatoes at 300° for 1 hour. Gently cut one end off each potato, ¾-inch from end (so that potato will stand up vertically). Cut remaining potato in two pieces, one piece ⅔ of the remaining potato and the other piece ⅓. The larger piece should be the piece with end cut off. Scoop out the two pieces, making sure not to penetrate the cut-off end. Add butter, salt, and pepper to scooped-out potato and mash well together. Put mixture in electric mixer and beat with whisk attachment, gradually adding buttermilk until mixture whips. (The exact amount of milk cannot be predetermined. It depends on amount of moisture in potatoes.) Stuff whipped potato mixture into skin of part of the potato with the end cut off. Pile up mixture as high as possible. Grease a baking sheet with the vegetable oil. Stand each potato up on end and bake at 400° for 25 minutes, or until brown on top.

Stand each potato on end to serve. (After all this trouble, whatever you do, don't lay them down.)

Sautéed Mushrooms

Serves 8

1/2 stick butter
2 garlic cloves, pressed
2 pounds medium-size mushrooms, cleaned and quartered
1 teaspoon salt
1/2 teaspoon black pepper

12-inch frying pan

Melt butter in frying pan on medium high. Add garlic, mushrooms, salt, and pepper. Sauté 5 minutes, or until mushrooms are tender and beginning to brown.

Cream Cheese Pie

This recipe came from Raven Graydon Tarpley (Mrs. Peter) of Columbia. She devised this marvelous, inexpensive, and delicious pie from her grandmother's cheese cake recipe. We made hundreds of these pies at Trinity Cathedral.

2 (9-inch) pies, 6 servings per pie

CRUST
1 1/2 cups graham cracker crumbs
  (about 12 graham crackers)
5 Tablespoons sugar
1 stick butter, melted
2 egg whites, lightly beaten until just foamy

Two (9-inch) pie pans

FILLING
3 (8-ounce) packages cream cheese,
  room temperature
1 cup sugar
3 eggs
1 stick butter, melted
1/2 teaspoon orange extract

Cream Cheese Pie for 168

CRUST
28 institutional graham cracker crumb crusts

FILLING
16 pounds cream cheese
10 3/4 cups sugar
32 eggs
2 3/4 pounds butter, melted
5 1/2 teaspoons orange extract

GARNISH
Shredded or grated semisweet chocolate or a twisted orange slice and a mint leaf on each serving

TO MAKE CRUST: Preheat regular oven to 450° or convection oven to 425°.

Mix graham cracker crumbs, sugar, and butter. Press into pie pans and brush with egg white. Bake in either oven for 5 minutes, or until golden brown. Cool 5 minutes.

TO MAKE FILLING: Beat cream cheese and sugar in electric mixer until fluffy. Beat in eggs one at a time (or four at a time for large recipe), scraping down sides between each addition. Add melted butter, continuing to beat slowly. Add orange extract and beat well. Divide filling between crusts. Bake in either oven 10 minutes, or until tops start to brown. Set in cool place for 4 hours before slicing. Garnish and serve. Refrigerate leftovers.

Broccoli
See page 143

French Bread
See page 139

Mid-Winter Graduation
Speakers Luncheon
The President's House
Six Glebe Street

COLLEGE OYSTERS
CROWN ROAST OF PORK WITH CRANBERRY DRESSING
WILD RICE WITH MUSHROOMS
GREEN BEANS WITH BENNE SEEDS
COLLEGE BISCUITS

SWEDISH CREAM
WITH
ORANGE-BRANDY SAUCE

ICED TEA
RED AND WHITE WINE
COFFEE

College Oysters

This is an elegant first course served in coquille shells or baking dishes. Place on top of salad-size plates covered with a layer of sea salt or fresh seaweed, which can be ordered from a seafood market.

Serves 8

48 oysters (drain oysters, reserve liquor, and set aside)

SPINACH
2 ½ pounds fresh spinach, washed, stemmed, and chopped
5 Tablespoons butter
1 ½ cups finely chopped green onions, including tops
¾ cup finely chopped parsley
¾ cup finely chopped celery
1 ½ garlic cloves, peeled and minced
¾ cup fresh fennel leaves, washed and chopped
Salt
Black pepper

WHITE SAUCE
5 Tablespoons butter
1 ½ Tablespoons flour
3 Tablespoons oyster liquor
¾ cup heavy whipping cream
Dash Worcestershire sauce
Dash Tabasco®, or to taste
1 cup freshly grated Parmesan cheese

TO MAKE SPINACH: Sauté spinach (p.3, omitting butter). Heat butter and sauté green onions, celery, parsley, garlic, and fennel leaves on medium high 3 to 5 minutes, or until tender. Add cooked spinach and sauté, stirring constantly, 1 minute. Take vegetables out of pan and set aside.

TO MAKE WHITE SAUCE: Add butter to same pan and heat on low. Blend in flour and cook slowly, stirring constantly, until smooth. Whisk in oyster liquor. When blended, whisk in cream, Worcestershire sauce, and Tabasco®.

Cook 1 to 2 minutes, or until creamy and smooth. Add vegetables and mix well.

TO ASSEMBLE: Preheat oven to 350°.

Place 6 oysters in each shell or baking dish and sprinkle with salt and pepper. Cover oysters with spinach mixture and sprinkle with Parmesan cheese. Bake at 350° for 25 minutes, or until oysters are curled around edges, spinach is hot, and cheese is brown. If cheese is not brown enough, run under broiler but watch carefully.

Crown Roast of Pork with Cranberry Dressing

Alex made this for the family when Zoe Caroline was christened thirty years ago. It's a real "crowd pleaser" when passed around the room before it's cut and served.

Serves 8, two ribs each with dressing

ROAST
16 ribs from the rib end of 2 pork loins, shaped into crown*
½ teaspoon salt
½ teaspoon pepper
8 peeled garlic cloves, sliced in half
½ teaspoon dried rosemary (or 1 ½ teaspoons fresh)

DRESSING
1 cup chopped sweet onion
2 Tablespoons butter
1 pound bulk mild sausage
1 ½ cups chopped celery
½ cup raisins
½ cup chopped fresh cranberries
2 tart apples, peeled and diced
½ teaspoon sage (or 1 ½ teaspoons fresh)
½ teaspoon thyme (or 1 ½ teaspoons fresh)
½ teaspoon rosemary (or 1 ½ teaspoons fresh)
½ teaspoon salt
½ teaspoon black pepper
4 cups fresh white bread crumbs
1 cup milk

Crown Roast of Pork with Cranberry Stuffing, Wild and Brown Rice with Mushrooms and Green Beans

Parsley or watercress
Cranberries for garnish

TO ROAST:
Sprinkle roast with salt and pepper. Cut slits between every 2 ribs and insert ½ garlic clove. Rub roast with rosemary. Bake at 325° in shallow baking pan until meat begins to pull away from ribs and a meat thermometer inserted into the thickest part of meat, but not touching the bone, registers 165° (approximately 20 minutes per pound). Stuff dressing into center of roast 1 hour before removal from oven.

TO MAKE DRESSING:
Sauté onions in butter. Brown sausage and crumble. Drain. Mix onions and sausage with celery, raisins, cranberries, apples, and seasonings. Sauté 5-7 minutes. Moisten bread with milk and squeeze dry. Combine all.

* Have butcher shape roast into a crown. This is a job for a professional. Put little chef caps on each rib after roast is done and garnish with parsley or watercress and fresh cranberries for color.

Wild Rice with Mushrooms

Serves 12

2 cups wild rice
6 cups chicken broth, fresh or canned
1 1/4 teaspoons salt
2 Tablespoons butter
2 large cloves garlic, minced
*1 pound medium-size mushrooms, cleaned and
    quartered*
1/2 teaspoon black pepper

3-quart heavy saucepan with lid
12-inch frying pan

Rinse wild rice in cold water 3 times. Tiny white specks will begin to show. Combine chicken broth, 1 teaspoon salt, and wild rice in saucepan. Cover and bring to a boil on high. Reduce to low and simmer 45 minutes, or until grains are opened and soft. If all of chicken broth has not been absorbed, drain well. Place in bowl and cover lightly with aluminum foil. Rice can be held at this point until ready to serve.

When ready to serve, heat butter in frying pan until hot but not smoking. Add garlic, mushrooms, remaining 1/4 teaspoon salt, and pepper. Sauté on medium high 3 or 4 minutes, or until garlic is golden brown and mushrooms are tender. Add wild rice and toss until hot.

Wild and Brown Rice

Serves 8

Combine half of the Wild Rice with Mushrooms recipe and half of Brown Rice recipe (p.26) and mix well. Toss on medium high until hot.

Green Beans with Benne Seeds

Small, smooth, thin green beans seem to be the most flavorful.

Serves 8

2 pounds green beans
1 Tablespoon butter
*1 teaspoon chopped fresh tarragon,
    or 1/2 teaspoon dried*
2 garlic cloves, peeled and pressed
1 teaspoon salt
Juice of 1/2 lemon (optional)
2 Tablespoons browned benne seeds*

12-inch frying pan

Wash beans and snap off ends. Steam in colander over boiling water 10 minutes, or until tender and almost done. Run cold water over beans to stop further cooking. At this point they may be set aside until ready to serve.

When ready to serve, heat butter in frying pan on medium. Add tarragon, garlic, and 1/2 teaspoon salt. Cook, stirring constantly, until tarragon and garlic are limp. Turn heat to high and add beans. Add lemon juice (optional), benne seeds and remaining 1/2 teaspoon salt. Cook beans, stirring constantly, 5 minutes, or until tender enough to satisfy your taste.

* To brown benne seeds, spread on baking sheet and bake at 350° for 10 minutes, or until golden brown. Watch carefully; they get too brown quickly.

Orange-Brandy Sauce for Swedish Cream

This sauce makes a fabulous winter accompaniment to the Swedish Cream. It is pretty and delicious. Don't chop the orange zest for this recipe. The long, thin strands are part of the design.

10 servings for Swedish Cream

½ cup brandy
1 hard-packed cup light brown sugar
¼ cup undiluted frozen orange juice
1 cup orange zest, not chopped
2 cups orange sections
   (about 6 top-grade, fresh navel oranges)
2 Tablespoons Grand Marnier® liqueur

Heat brandy in saucepan. When it starts to bubble on top, light with a match or gas lighter. When flame has disappeared, add sugar and frozen orange juice and stir to combine. Heat until sugar has melted. Remove from heat and add orange zest. Cool, cover, and refrigerate until ready to use.

Gently toss orange sections with Grand Marnier® just before serving. Place 5 orange sections around each Swedish Cream. Spoon some of sauce and zest over each and serve.

Swedish Cream
See page 4

College Biscuits
See page 3

Holiday Drop-In
The President's House
Six Glebe Street

AMARETTO HOT CHOCOLATE
WITH
MARSHMALLOWS OR SOFT WHIPPED CREAM

CRANBERRY-APPLE HOLIDAY PUNCH

GINGER COOKIES
HOLIDAY BUTTER COOKIES
CHOCOLATE FUDGE COOKIES
CHOCOLATE PEANUT BUTTER COOKIES
SANDIES

Amaretto Hot Chocolate

This hot chocolate is good enough to be dessert. You can top it with whipped cream or marshmallows.

Serves 8

8 Tablespoons sugar
8 Tablespoons cocoa
2 quarts milk
2 teaspoons pure vanilla extract
8 ounces amaretto liqueur, or to taste

Mix sugar and cocoa in saucepan. Stir in 1 cup milk. Add vanilla and remaining milk and mix well. Heat on low until hot but not boiling to prevent curdling. Add amaretto and serve.

Soft Whipped Cream

$\frac{1}{2}$ pint heavy whipping cream
2 Tablespoons sugar
$\frac{1}{2}$ teaspoon pure vanilla extract

Combine cream, sugar, and vanilla in electric mixer and whip to soft peaks.

Cranberry-Apple Holiday Punch

15 (4-ounce) servings

1 quart cranberry juice
5 $\frac{1}{3}$ cups apple juice
3 Tablespoons light brown sugar
1 $\frac{1}{2}$ teaspoons whole cloves
2 sticks cinnamon

3-quart saucepan with lid

Mix cranberry juice, apple juice, sugar, cloves, and cinnamon. Bring to a boil, reduce to low and simmer, partially covered, 30 minutes. Strain or dip out cloves and cinnamon. Serve hot.

NOTE: This punch can be made ahead, refrigerated for 2 to 3 days, and reheated when ready to serve.

200 (4-ounce) servings

2 gallons + 3 quarts cranberry juice
3 $\frac{1}{2}$ gallons apple juice
1 pound light brown sugar
1 $\frac{1}{4}$ ounces whole cloves
12 sticks cinnamon

Put cranberry juice and apple juice in large electric coffee maker. Put sugar, cloves, and cinnamon in basket without a filter. Perk for 1 hour, or until ready light comes on. Serve hot.

Ginger Cookies

10 dozen

1 $\frac{1}{2}$ sticks margarine, room temperature
1 cup sugar
1 egg
$\frac{1}{4}$ cup molasses
2 cups all-purpose flour
$\frac{1}{2}$ Tablespoon baking soda
1 teaspoon cinnamon
1 teaspoon ground cloves
1 Tablespoon ground ginger
2 teaspoons peeled, finely chopped fresh ginger
$\frac{1}{2}$ cup chopped pecans, toasted
1 cup currants

Sugar for rolling balls of dough

Approximately 650

9 sticks margarine, room temperature
6 cups sugar
6 eggs, lightly beaten
1 $\frac{1}{2}$ cups molasses
12 cups all-purpose flour
3 Tablespoons baking soda
2 Tablespoons cinnamon

2 Tablespoons ground cloves
6 Tablespoons ground ginger
3 Tablespoons peeled, finely chopped
  fresh ginger
3 cups chopped pecans, toasted
6 cups currants

Cream margarine and sugar in electric mixer on medium until light and fluffy. Add egg and molasses and beat until well blended. Mix flour, baking soda, cinnamon, cloves, and ground ginger. Add to margarine and sugar mixture and beat on medium until well blended. Add fresh ginger, pecans, and currants and stir by hand. Cover and refrigerate 3 hours, or freeze for future baking.

When ready to bake, preheat regular oven to 350° or a convection oven to 325°. Pinch off teaspoons of dough and roll into balls the size of a quarter. Drop balls of dough into sugar and roll around to cover. Place two inches apart on baking sheets. Bake in either oven 8 to 10 minutes, or until lightly browned. Remove cookies from baking sheets and cool. They will keep for several weeks if stored in a tightly covered container. As they age they become more flavorful.

Holiday Butter Cookies

These cookies are good anytime, with or without "sprinkles"!

4 dozen

1 stick butter
½ cup sugar
1 teaspoon pure vanilla extract
1 egg yolk
1 cup all-purpose flour
1 Tablespoon red "sprinkles"
1 Tablespoon green "sprinkles"

Preheat oven to 325°.

Cream butter and sugar in electric mixer. Beat in vanilla and egg yolk. Gradually beat in flour. Pinch off pieces of dough and roll into balls about the size of a quarter. Place on baking sheets. Gently press with hand to level tops. They will be about ½-inch high. Sprinkle half of cookies with red "sprinkles" and half with green "sprinkles." Bake cookies at 325° for 12 to 15 minutes, or until very lightly browned. Cool at room temperature.

Chocolate Fudge Cookies

Marlene Addlestone (Mrs. Nathan) and her husband of Charleston are great supporters of the College. These are her special fudge cookies.

8 dozen

COOKIES
1 stick butter
2 squares unsweetened chocolate, chopped
1 egg
1 cup light brown sugar
1 teaspoon pure vanilla extract
¼ teaspoon salt
½ teaspoon baking soda
1 ⅔ cups all-purpose flour
½ cup sour cream

FROSTING
1 stick butter
3 ¾ cups confectioners' sugar
¾ cup cocoa, sifted
1 ½ teaspoons pure vanilla extract
⅓ cup milk

33 dozen

COOKIES
1 pound butter
8 squares unsweetened chocolate, chopped
4 eggs
4 cups light brown sugar
1 Tablespoon + 1 teaspoon pure vanilla extract
1 teaspoon salt

2 teaspoons baking soda
6⅔ cups all-purpose flour
2 cups sour cream

FROSTING
1 pound butter
15 cups confectioners' sugar
3 cups cocoa, sifted
2 Tablespoons pure vanilla extract
1⅓ cups milk

TO MAKE COOKIES: Preheat regular oven to 350° or convection oven to 325°. Spray baking sheets with vegetable spray.

Melt butter and chocolate in top of double boiler over, but not touching, simmering water. Combine egg, brown sugar, and vanilla in electric mixer and mix well. Combine salt, baking soda, and flour and mix well. Add melted butter and chocolate to egg and sugar mixture and mix well. Add flour mixture and stir. Add sour cream. Mix until well blended. Drop cookie dough by half teaspoonfuls (about the size of a quarter) 1 inch apart onto baking sheets. Bake 4 minutes in either oven. Leave on baking sheets to cool and frost. These cookies are so light and small that the least bit of overcooking will dry them out.

TO MAKE FROSTING: Melt butter. Add sugar, cocoa, and vanilla and mix well. Gradually stir in milk to make a smooth frosting. Swirl frosting onto cookie with tip of spoon. It will make a pretty pattern with a little point in the center.

Chocolate Peanut Butter Cookies

Lillian Arrants (Mrs. Willard) of Lexington gave us this recipe. The key to the success of these delicious cookies is using good quality chocolate. We use Ghirardelli®, which is made for eating as well as baking.

5 dozen

1 (4-stack) box Ritz® Crackers
14½ ounces crunchy peanut butter
2 pounds semisweet chocolate, chopped

Long metal icing spatula

20 dozen

4 (4-stack) boxes Ritz® Crackers
6 pounds + 2 ounces crunchy peanut butter
7 pounds semisweet chocolate, chopped

Spread half of crackers with peanut butter, being careful to keep peanut butter from spreading over the edge of cracker. Top with remaining crackers.

TO TEMPER CHOCOLATE: Place chocolate in double boiler over hot, but not boiling, water until it begins to melt. Turn heat off and let chocolate continue to melt over hot water, stirring occasionally. Pour melted chocolate on marble or tile slab or on the back of a baking sheet. Scrape chocolate back and forth with icing spatula until it begins to cool and thicken. Put chocolate back into top of double boiler, but *not* over warm water, and continue to stir with spatula until it cools to just below body temperature. Test by putting a little chocolate on your lip; it should feel cool. The chocolate should have the consistency of thick pudding.

Using a small pair of tongs, dip each peanut butter cracker "sandwich" in melted chocolate, being sure to submerge it enough to be completely covered. Hold "sandwich" over pot and scrape extra chocolate off with icing spatula, leaving a smooth chocolate covering on top, bottom, and around edge. Place chocolate-covered "sandwiches" on wax paper until chocolate hardens. May be refrigerated to speed up hardening.

The drawing room at Six Glebe decorated for the holidays

61

Simons Guild Holiday
Luncheon
Garden Room
The President's House
Six Glebe Street

COLLEGE CHICKEN AND BROCCOLI GRATIN
CRANBERRY SALAD
WITH
HOMEMADE MAYONNAISE
COLLEGE BISCUITS

GINGERBREAD WITH LEMON SAUCE

ICED TEA
COFFEE

College Chicken and Broccoli Gratin

Serves 8

2 (3 ½ to 4-pound) whole baked chickens
  (p.138)
2 heads cooked broccoli (p.143)
Juice of 1 lemon
6 ½ cups white sauce
1 (8-ounce) can sliced water chestnuts, washed
  and drained
1 cup seasoned bread crumbs

9 x 13 baking dish lightly sprayed with
  vegetable spray

WHITE SAUCE
4 cups heavy whipping cream
2 cups of the juices and drippings from baking
  pan of chicken, fat skimmed off
6 Tablespoons butter
9 Tablespoons all-purpose flour
2 teaspoons salt
1 Tablespoon fresh lemon juice
2 teaspoons curry powder

Heavy-bottomed 3-quart saucepan

SEASONED BREAD CRUMBS
3 slices white bread, toasted and processed into
  fine crumbs
1 Tablespoon butter
½ clove garlic, pressed
½ teaspoon sage
¼ teaspoon salt

TO MAKE WHITE SAUCE: Combine 4 cups of whipping cream with chicken juices and bring to a boil. Heat butter on low. Blend in flour and cook, whisking constantly, until mixture begins to foam. Whisk and cook 2 minutes longer. Remove from heat. When butter and flour mixture stops foaming, add boiling cream and chicken juices. Stir with whisk to blend, and cook 2 or 3 minutes on medium high, or until mixture comes to a boil. Boil 2 minutes, stirring with whisk. Reduce heat to a simmer, add salt, lemon juice, and curry powder and stir with whisk 10 minutes, or until thick.

TO MAKE SEASONED BREAD CRUMBS: Melt butter in a saucepan. Add garlic, sage, and salt. Stir until blended and cook on low until garlic is soft and begins to brown. Add toasted bread crumbs and mix well.

TO ASSEMBLE: Preheat regular oven to 350° or convection oven to 325°.

Pull meat off chicken in approximately 2-inch pieces, but use all meat no matter how small. Layer bottom of dish with chicken. Pour three cups white sauce over chicken. Layer cooked broccoli over white sauce. Drizzle lemon juice over broccoli. Layer water chestnuts. Spread remaining white sauce over water chestnuts. Sprinkle seasoned bread crumbs on top.

Bake in either oven 1 hour. Let set for 30 minutes before serving.

NOTE: Can be refrigerated or frozen. Thaw and bring to room temperature before reheating in either oven for 1 hour, or until hot.

Gingerbread with Lemon Sauce

This recipe originated with Georgia Herbert (Mrs. Beverly) of Columbia, Marion Sullivan's great-aunt.

8 large or 12 small servings

1 stick butter, room temperature
½ cup dark brown sugar
1 egg
2 ½ cups all-purpose flour
1 ½ teaspoons baking soda
2 teaspoons ground ginger
1 teaspoon ground cloves
½ teaspoon salt
1 cup molasses
1 cup hot water

Lemon Sauce
9 x 9 x 2 baking pan, greased

Preheat oven to 350°.

Cream butter and sugar in electric mixer until light and fluffy. Add egg and beat until light in color. Mix flour, baking soda, ginger, cloves, and salt. Mix molasses and hot water. Whisk flour mixture and molasses mixture into butter mixture by hand, alternating dry and liquid ingredients, beginning and ending with dry.

Bake at 350° for 40 minutes, or until cake tester comes out clean. Cool in pan. Can be made the day before. Serve with Lemon Sauce.

Gingerbread for 96

96 large pieces or (120 small)

2 institutional-size boxes Pillsbury
    Gingerbread Mix
Two (18 x 26) pans

Follow directions on box, using water only. Bake as directed. Cut each cake 6 x 8. Gingerbread can be served warm from pans. If serving at room temperature, cool in pans. Serve with dollop of Soft Whipped Cream (p.58) or with Lemon Sauce.

Lemon Sauce

8 servings for gingerbread

$\frac{1}{2}$ cup sugar
1 Tablespoon cornstarch
1 cup water
2 Tablespoons fresh lemon juice
  (about 2 lemons)
1 teaspoon lemon zest
3 Tablespoons cold butter

96 servings for gingerbread

6 cups sugar
12 Tablespoons cornstarch
12 cups water
1 $\frac{1}{2}$ cups fresh lemon juice
4 Tablespoons finely chopped
  lemon zest
4 $\frac{1}{2}$ sticks butter

Combine sugar, cornstarch, and water in top of double boiler over, but not touching, simmering water and stir gently 20 to 25 minutes, or until thick enough to coat spoon. Remove from heat and stir in lemon juice, lemon zest, and cold butter. Serve warm or at room temperature. Sauce thickens as it cools.

Lemon Sauce will keep refrigerated for 3 days. When ready to serve, warm in double boiler.

Cranberry Salad
See page 133

Homemade Mayonnaise
See page 127

College Biscuits
See page 3

*Faculty and Staff
Holiday Party
Willard A. Silcox
Gymnasium*

A SMORGASBORD
including special desserts

BROWNIES
RASPBERRY TRIFLE
LEMON SQUARES
SUGAR COOKIES
CARAMEL DIP FOR APPLES

WINE
COFFEE

Brownies

Marion Sullivan created this popular dessert from the brownie recipe of our friend Gloria Burg of Columbia. Marion made them twice as thick and added a dark European icing that makes them rich and creamy.

48 bite-size brownies

BROWNIES
2 sticks butter
¾ cup cocoa powder
1 cup all-purpose flour
1 teaspoon baking powder
½ teaspoon salt
4 eggs
2 cups sugar
1 ½ teaspoons pure vanilla extract
1 cup chopped pecans

9 x 13 x 2 pan

ICING
½ cup heavy whipping cream
½ pound semisweet chocolate chips

1-quart saucepan

TO MAKE BROWNIES: Preheat oven to 300°. Line pan with aluminum foil, leaving 2 inches of foil extending over edges.

Melt butter and add cocoa, whisking to remove lumps. Set aside. Sift flour, baking powder, and salt. Set aside. Beat eggs, sugar, and vanilla in electric mixer on low to mix well. Mix in half the flour mixture and half the cocoa mixture. Repeat with other halves, blending well to remove lumps. Fold in nuts by hand and spread batter into pan. Bake at 300° for 30 to 35 minutes, or until edges begin to pull away from sides of pan. Lift brownies out of pan using edges of foil. Cool to room temperature before icing.

TO MAKE ICING: Bring the cream to a boil on medium. Remove from heat and whisk in chocolate chips until smooth. Spread warm icing over top of uncut brownies. Refrigerate until set. Cut 6 x 8 for bite-size pieces.

Raspberry Trifle

A good brand of store-bought pound cake works fine in trifle. If you use homemade cake, you will find that a dry pound cake or leftover pound cake will soak up the sherry better than a fresh, moist cake.

Serves 10 to 12

1 pound Cream Cheese Pound Cake
  (recipe follows)
1 cup dry sherry
2 cups heavy whipping cream
2 teaspoons pure vanilla extract
6 Tablespoons sugar
3 cups Custard (recipe follows)
½ cup sliced almonds, toasted
1 quart fresh raspberries

8 x 12 x 2 pan
3-quart clear glass bowl

Cut pound cake into approximately 1 ½-inch squares. Place squares in pan and pour sherry over cake in order for each piece to absorb sherry.

Whip cream, vanilla, and sugar in electric mixer until thick, but not stiff, and forms soft peaks. Reserve ½ cup whipped cream for top layer. Mix remaining cream with custard until completely blended. To layer trifle, begin and end with custard and cream mixture. Reserve 1 cup raspberries for top. Make 4 layers of custard, cake, almonds, and raspberries. End with layer of custard. Spread reserved ½ cup whipped cream over custard and garnish with reserved raspberries. Cover and refrigerate 12 hours before serving to allow custard and cream to soak into cake.

NOTE: A pint of strawberries makes a great substitute when raspberries are out of season. Wash strawberries, reserve a few whole ones for top, and quarter remainder.

Cream Cheese Pound Cake

This recipe came from Willie Ewing Crockett (Mrs. James) of Vidalia, Ga.

Serves 16 slices

1 Tablespoon butter, room temperature
Flour for preparing pan
Large tube pan (10-inch wide x 4-inch deep)

3 sticks butter, room temperature
8 ounces cream cheese, room temperature
3 cups sugar
3 cups cake flour, sifted twice before measuring
6 eggs
2 teaspoons pure vanilla extract
½ cup + 2 teaspoons cocoa (optional)

Position oven shelves with one on bottom and one in center. Preheat oven to 300°. Grease and flour pan, using the Tablespoon of butter.

Cream butter and cheese in electric mixer on medium. Add sugar gradually and beat 15 to 20 minutes, or until light and fluffy. Add flour, ½ cup at a time, alternating with 1 egg at a time, beginning and ending with flour. Mix well between each addition. Add cocoa (optional). Beat in vanilla and pour into pan.

Place pan of water on bottom shelf of oven. Place tube pan in middle of center shelf. Bake at 300° degrees for 1½ hours, or until cake tester comes out clean. Cool cake in pan for 1 hour. Turn out onto cake plate, cool completely, cover airtight, and store overnight to improve flavor.

NOTE: All-purpose flour can be used in this recipe, but the cake will be much heavier.

Add cocoa for chocolate pound cake.

Custard

Alex's mother, Ret Sanders (Mrs. Alex M., Sr.), has made this custard for friends and family members over the years when they were sick. It's always delivered in a mason jar and it's always delicious!

3 cups or Trifle for 10 to 12

3 eggs
5 rounded Tablespoons sugar
3 cups milk
2 teaspoons pure vanilla extract

Whisk eggs and sugar together in top of double boiler off heat. Scald milk on medium until hot but not boiling. Whisk ¼ cup scalded milk into egg mixture. Whisk in remaining hot milk.

Place top of double boiler over, but not touching, simmering water. Continue to stir with whisk for 15 to 18 minutes, or until thick enough to coat a spoon. Whisk in vanilla. Cool, cover, and refrigerate until ready to use.

NOTE: Watch custard carefully during thickening process. It can quickly overcook and curdle. This may happen the first time you try to make it. Custard will thicken as it cools (and even more when you refrigerate it).

Shortcut Raspberry Trifle

Barbara Streett (Mrs. Richard M., Sr.) of Columbia discovered these shortcuts for making trifle for large groups. It's delicious and very easy to make.

Trifle for 10 to 12

1 pound of pound cake
1 cup dry sherry
2 cups heavy whipping cream
2 teaspoons pure vanilla extract
6 Tablespoons sugar
1 large package vanilla Jell-O® Instant
  Pudding and Pie Filling
3 cups half-and-half
½ cup sliced almonds, toasted
1 quart fresh raspberries

8 x 12 x 2 pan

3-quart clear glass bowl

Trifle for 30

3 pounds of pound cake
3 cups dry sherry
6 cups heavy whipping cream
3 Tablespoons pure vanilla extract
1 ¼ cups sugar
3 large packages vanilla Jell-O® Instant
  Pudding and Pie Filling
4 ½ pints half-and-half
1 ½ cups sliced almonds, toasted
3 quarts fresh raspberries

Three (8 x 12 x 2) pans
Glass punch bowl

Cut pound cake into 1 ½-inch squares. Place in pan and pour sherry over cake in order for each piece to absorb sherry. Whip cream, vanilla, and sugar in electric mixer until thick, but not stiff, and forms soft peaks. Reserve ½ cup for top layer. Combine pudding mix and half-and-half in electric mixer and whip on low 2 minutes. Stir in whipping cream until completely blended.

To layer trifle, begin and end with pudding mixture. Reserve 1 cup raspberries for top. Make 4 layers of pudding, cake, almonds, and raspberries. Spread top with reserved ½ cup whipped cream and garnish with reserved raspberries. Cover trifle and refrigerate 12 hours before serving to allow pudding to soak into cake.

NOTE: A pint (three pints for large recipe) of strawberries makes a great substitute when raspberries are out of season. Wash strawberries, reserve a few whole ones for top, and quarter the remainder.

Lemon Squares

The College's chef, Lee Godbey, has this recipe down to a science.

24 (2-inch) squares

CRUST
2 sticks butter
2 cups all-purpose flour
½ cup confectioners' sugar

9 x 13 x 2 pan

FILLING
2 cups sugar
4 Tablespoons all-purpose flour
2 teaspoons baking powder
¼ teaspoon salt
4 eggs, lightly beaten
½ cup fresh lemon juice
4 teaspoons finely chopped lemon zest
Confectioners' sugar

TO MAKE CRUST: Preheat oven to 350°. Line pan with aluminum foil, leaving 2 inches of foil extending over edges. Spray foil with vegetable spray.

Combine butter, flour, and confectioners' sugar in electric mixer and blend well. Pat dough into pan as evenly as possible. Bake crust at 350° for 30 minutes, or until golden brown.

TO MAKE FILLING: While crust is baking, combine sugar, flour, baking powder, and salt in electric mixer on low. Add eggs, lemon juice, and lemon zest and mix well. Pour mixture over baked crust. Bake at 350° for 30 minutes, or until golden brown.

Leave lemon squares in pan to cool. Cover and refrigerate overnight. Lift out of pan using edges of foil. Cut 4 x 6 for 2-inch squares (or 6 x 8 for bite-size squares). Sift confectioners' sugar over tops when ready to serve. Freeze well.

Caramel Dip for Apples
See page 141

New Year's Day Dinner
The Kitchen
The President's House
Six Glebe Street

OYSTER STEW

ROASTED PORK LOIN
HOPPIN' JOHN
COLLARDS WITH CHOPS
WHIPPED SWEET POTATOES

APPLESAUCE WITH HORSERADISH
ARTICHOKE PICKLE

SKILLET CORN BREAD

APPLE PIE

ICED TEA
ROSÉ WINE

Oyster Stew

Serve as a first course or for lunch with a salad. Oyster crackers are an essential with this stew.

10 (8-ounce) servings

2 sticks butter
½ cup chopped jumbo yellow onion
12 Tablespoons all-purpose flour
2 quarts milk, scalded
2 pints select oysters and liquor
1 Tablespoon + 1 teaspoon Worcestershire
  sauce
¼ teaspoon Tabasco®
1 Tablespoon salt, or to taste
1 teaspoon black pepper
½ teaspoon sugar (if oysters are not sweet)

3-gallon pot

Melt butter in pot on low. Add onions and sauté 3-4 minutes, or until soft and translucent. Remove onions and reserve.

Whisk flour into butter mixture. Cook, whisking, 5 minutes, or until there are no flour lumps and mixture has thickened. Whisk in milk, Worcestershire sauce, Tabasco®, salt, pepper, and sugar if desired. Stir in oysters in their liquor and cook on low, partially covered, whisking occasionally 15 minutes, or until hot. Do not let stew simmer or boil; it will curdle and separate. Remove from heat. Reheat on low when ready to serve.

Roasted Pork Loin

This was Tootie Williams' (John W.) recipe and now is Reece Williams' New Year's Day Special!

Serves 8

Whole bone-in pork loin, with chine bone
  removed*
2 teaspoons salt

2 teaspoons black pepper
8 peeled garlic cloves, sliced in half
1 teaspoon rosemary (or 1 Tablespoon fresh)

Sprinkle roast with salt and pepper. Cut 16 slits in loin, equal distance apart, and insert garlic. Rub roast with rosemary. Bake at 325° in shallow baking pan until meat begins to pull away from bone and internal temperature is 165° (approximately 30 minutes per pound).

* Have the butcher remove the chine bone unless you really know what you are doing.

Hoppin' John

Serves 8 to 10

1 cup dried cow or field peas
6 cups water
3 teaspoons salt
¼ teaspoon black pepper
1 (12-ounce) ham hock
1 slice thick-sliced bacon
2 cups chopped jumbo yellow onion
1 cup Uncle Ben's Converted® White Rice

3-quart saucepan, 12-inch frying pan, 1½-quart heavy saucepan, and 3-quart baking dish

Combine peas, water, 2 teaspoons salt, pepper, and ham hock in 3-quart saucepan and bring to a boil on high. Reduce to low, cover partially, and cook peas for 45 minutes, or until soft but not mushy. Set aside covered.

Fry bacon in frying pan until all fat is rendered. Makes about 3 Tablespoons of fat. Discard bacon and reserve fat. Pull skin and all membrane from ham hock. Reserve meat. Combine skin and membrane in frying pan and fry on low until all fat is rendered. Discard skin and membrane. Combine bacon fat with ham fat, add onions, and cook on low 15 minutes, or until onions are clear and soft. Set aside.

Combine 2 cups broth from peas, remaining teaspoon salt, and rice in 1½-quart saucepan. Bring to a boil on high, reduce to simmer on very low, and cook 25 to 30 minutes, or until all liquid is absorbed. A spoon slipped down the side to the bottom should come up with almost dry rice. Fluff with fork.

Preheat oven to 350°.

Peas should have soaked up remaining broth. Shred reserved meat from ham hock and mix with reserved onions and fat. Combine with rice in 3-quart baking dish. Cover and heat at 350° for 15 to 20 minutes, or until hot.

NOTE: Hoppin' John can be made a day ahead and refrigerated overnight. Remove from refrigerator 1 hour before reheating at 350° for 30 minutes, or until hot.

Collards with Chops

Serves 10 to 12

*2 pounds thinly sliced pork chops (about ⅓-
inch to ½-inch thick)*
2 teaspoons salt
2 large bunches collard greens
¼ to ½ teaspoon sugar (optional)

3-gallon pot with lid

Wash pork chops and layer on bottom of pot. Cover chops with water and add salt. Bring water to a boil on high, cover pot, and reduce to low. Cut leaves from each side of stems, discard stems, and drop leaves in sink filled with cold water. Shake leaves in water, allowing dirt, sand, and trash to fall to bottom. Tear leaves apart with hands and wash again. Taking leaves by handfuls, shake off water and place in pot with chops. Cover and cook on low for 1 hour. Add sugar and more salt if desired. If meat on chops is falling off bones, take bones out and mix meat with collards. If not, remove chops and serve as a meat dish. Simmer collards 15 minutes, or until tender.

Whipped Sweet Potatoes

Peggy Ashby, the House Manager at the President's House, gave us this recipe.

Serves 8

7 pounds sweet potatoes, washed
2 sticks butter, diced
2 teaspoons salt
¼ teaspoon nutmeg
¼ cup fresh orange juice

1-quart baking dish or 12 orange shells*

Preheat oven to 425°. Line baking sheet with aluminum foil.

Place potatoes on baking sheet and bake at 425° for 30 minutes. Pierce several times with a fork and continue to bake 1½ hours, or until tender when pierced with a fork.

Scoop potatoes out of skins into bowl of electric mixer. Mash by hand with a potato masher. Beat in butter, salt, nutmeg, and orange juice until light and fluffy.

Transfer to baking dish or mound in orange shells. Can be set aside at this point. When ready to serve, bake at 350° for 20 minutes, or until hot.

* To make orange shells, wash oranges and cut in half. Remove fruit and tough membrane section, being careful not to pierce shell or pull stem center out, leaving a hole. Cut membrane away from center with scissors. Set fruit aside. Squeeze juice from membrane and shell. Discard membrane. Remove seeds. You should have the quarter cup of juice needed to add to the sweet potatoes.

Applesauce with Horseradish

2 cups

2 cups applesauce
2 Tablespoons prepared horseradish
⅛ teaspoon nutmeg

Combine ingredients and serve or refrigerate.

Apple Pie

This is Alex's secret apple pie trick. Thus ends the secret!

Serves 8

1 (9-inch) frozen Mrs. Smith's® Family-size
  Deep Dish Apple Pie
1 Tablespoon butter, room temperature
½ teaspoon cinnamon
¼ teaspoon nutmeg
1 egg, lightly beaten
1 Tablespoon sugar
1 pint vanilla ice cream or Soft Whipped Cream
(p.58)

Preheat oven to 350°.

Let pie thaw 15 minutes at room temperature. Carefully remove top crust with a knife. Spread soft butter over apples. Sprinkle with cinnamon and nutmeg.

Put top back on and crimp edges together as you would a homemade crust, or cut crust in strips and weave across top of filling like lattice. Brush top with beaten egg, being careful not to let it puddle. Sprinkle with sugar.

Bake pie at 350° for 1 hour, or until crust is golden brown. Let set 20 minutes before cutting. Serve with ice cream or Soft Whipped Cream (p.58).

Artichoke Pickle
See page 127

Skillet Corn Bread
See page 14

Academic Affairs Breakfast
Faculty House
Twenty Glebe Street

ORANGE JUICE
FRESH FRUIT

COUNTRY HAM
WITH
COLLEGE BISCUITS

SHRIMP AND GRAVY
WITH
STONE-GROUND GRITS
OR
MUSHROOM STRATA
WITH
BACON

SLICED TOMATOES IN SEASON

WHOLE WHEAT TOAST
COFFEE CAKE

COFFEE

Shrimp and Gravy

This recipe is served with Stone-Ground Grits. It's one of the most popular dishes in the Lowcountry. I've seen it served for breakfast, lunch, and dinner, but we like it best for breakfast or for supper on a chilly Sunday night.

Serves 8

6 slices bacon, diced
1 ½ cups finely diced red onion
½ cup finely diced green pepper
3 Tablespoons butter
6 Tablespoons all-purpose flour
4 cups chicken broth, fresh or canned
1 ½ teaspoons Kitchen Bouquet®
½ teaspoon Worcestershire sauce
½ teaspoon salt
¼ teaspoon black pepper
2 pounds medium shrimp, peeled and deveined

3-quart saucepan
12-inch frying pan

Brown bacon in saucepan on medium. Drain on paper towels and reserve. Add onions to hot fat and sauté on medium 2 minutes, or until soft. Add peppers and cook 5 minutes, stirring occasionally and scraping the brown bits off bottom of saucepan. Stir in 1 Tablespoon butter. Add flour and reduce to low. Stir until well mixed with vegetables and cook 5 minutes, or until lightly browned. Whisk in chicken broth until mixture is smooth. Increase heat to high and bring to a boil, whisking. Reduce to low and simmer 5 minutes, whisking occasionally. Add Kitchen Bouquet®, Worcestershire sauce, salt, pepper, and reserved bacon. Stir and simmer on low 20 to 30 minutes, or until reduced to about 2½ cups. At this point, the gravy can be refrigerated or frozen.

When ready to serve, thaw gravy, if necessary, and warm. Heat remaining 2 Tablespoons of butter in frying pan on medium high. When butter is hot, add shrimp. You may need to add them in 2 batches. Sauté shrimp 3 to 5 minutes, or until they curl and turn pink. Add to gravy and serve with hot grits.

Stone-Ground Grits

These are Alex's grits. Lowcountry water makes them taste better. If you don't live there, baking soda helps to reproduce that taste.

Serves 8

2 cups stone-ground grits
6 cups boiling water
2 teaspoons salt
¼ teaspoon baking soda
½ stick butter
1 cup milk
½ cup half-and-half

Pour grits into boiling water, with salt and baking soda. Reduce to simmer and cook 10 minutes, stirring often. Add butter and milk, and cook 5 minutes. Add half-and-half and cook very slowly 20-25 minutes, stirring often and adding more water if necessary to maintain correct consistency (thick but not runny). May be held in top of double boiler until ready to serve.

Mushroom Strata

This was first served to us by Ellen Smith (Mrs. John Hamilton) of Summerville.

Serves 6 to 8

4 cups 1-inch cubes French bread
2 Tablespoons butter
3 cups sliced fresh mushrooms (8 ounces)
1 cup chopped green onions, tops only
1 cup grated extra sharp cheddar cheese
1 cup grated colby cheese
6 eggs
3 Tablespoons Dijon mustard

1 ½ teaspoons salt
1 teaspoon black pepper
3 cups milk
½ teaspoon paprika

8 slices bacon, cooked, drained, and
     crumbled (optional)

9 x 13 (3-quart) baking dish, greased

Place cubes of bread in baking dish. Heat butter in saucepan on medium high. Add mushrooms and sauté 2 minutes, or until soft. Add green onions and sauté 30 seconds, or until wilted. Spread mushrooms, onions, and their juices over bread. Sprinkle cheese over all. Whisk eggs, mustard, salt, pepper, and milk together and pour over mixture in baking dish. Cover dish with plastic wrap and refrigerate overnight, or for at least 4 hours.

When ready to bake, preheat oven to 325°. Sprinkle paprika over top. Bake at 325° for 1 hour, or until browned.

Coffee Cake

Patty King (Mrs. L. Richardson) of Davidson, N.C. gave us this recipe. We like to make two of these cakes, mixing them one at a time. Put one in the center of a large serving plate; slice the other, and place the slices around the uncut cake. A flower or a small bouquet of flowers in a tiny container like a jigger can be placed in the center. The uncut cake can be frozen for a later occasion.

Serves 24 slices

CAKE
1 Tablespoon butter, room temperature
Flour for flouring pan
Bundt pan

2 sticks butter, room temperature
2 cups sugar
2 eggs

1 teaspoon pure vanilla extract
1 cup sour cream
2 cups all-purpose flour
1 teaspoon baking powder
¼ teaspoon salt

TOPPING
4 Tablespoons dark brown sugar
1 teaspoon cinnamon
1 cup chopped pecans, toasted

TO MAKE CAKE: Preheat oven to 350°. Grease and flour pan using the Tablespoon of butter.

Cream butter in electric mixer on medium. Gradually add sugar and beat 10 minutes, or until light and fluffy. Add eggs one at a time and beat 10 minutes after each. Beating gives this cake a light, fine texture.

Mix vanilla and sour cream. Combine flour, baking powder, and salt. Add flour mixture to butter and sugar in four parts, alternating with sour cream, beginning and ending with flour until all is well blended.

TO MAKE TOPPING: Mix brown sugar, cinnamon, and nuts.

TO ASSEMBLE: Spoon half of batter by Tablespoonfuls into pan. Spread batter evenly in pan and make a trough through the center of the batter with back of teaspoon. Spoon ¾ of topping into trough to prevent topping from sticking to sides. Spoon in remaining batter and sprinkle remaining topping over batter.

Bake at 350° for 55 minutes, or until cake tester comes out clean. Cool to room temperature before removing from pan. Freezes well.

Country Ham
See page 36

College Biscuits
See page 3

Whole Wheat Toast
See Homemade Loaf Bread page 102

School of the Arts Dinner
Faculty House
Twenty Glebe Street

GRAPEFRUIT AND AVOCADO SALAD
WITH FRUIT SALAD DRESSING

DUCK À L'ORANGE
WILD RICE WITH MUSHROOMS
OYSTER PIE
ASPARAGUS
SPOONBREAD

CHOCOLATE PIE
WITH
RASPBERRY SAUCE
AND
SOFT WHIPPED CREAM

Duck à l'Orange

This is Lee Godbey's recipe.

Serves 8 (½ duck each)

DUCK
4 (4 ½ to 5 pound) ducks
Salt
24 whole cloves
2 oranges, halved

SAUCE
8 teaspoons cornstarch
½ cup + 2 Tablespoons brandy
1 cup light brown sugar
2 cups orange juice
⅓ cup undiluted frozen orange juice
2 Tablespoons finely chopped shallots
1 large clove garlic, peeled and crushed
½ cup Grand Marnier®
3 Tablespoons orange zest
1 teaspoon fresh lemon juice

TO ROAST DUCK: Preheat oven to 325°.

Prick skin of ducks with tines of a sharp meat fork. Sprinkle inside and out with salt. Place ducks in shallow roasting pan breast side up. Press 6 cloves into each orange half and place in cavity of each duck. Tie legs together with string. Tuck wing tips under. Bake ducks at 325° for 1 ½ hours, or until golden brown. Leg joints should move freely when string is removed. Set aside for 45 minutes. Remove leg and thigh quarters from backbone in one piece. Remove wing and breast meat from rib bones in one piece. This will give a breast and leg quarter for each guest.

TO MAKE SAUCE: Dissolve cornstarch in 2 Tablespoons of brandy. Melt sugar in saucepan on low. Add orange juice, undiluted frozen orange juice, shallots, garlic, Grand Marnier®, and remaining ½ cup brandy. Bring to a boil, add dissolved cornstarch, and whisk to remove lumps. Simmer 5 minutes, or

until thick. While sauce is simmering, poach orange zest 2 minutes in enough water to cover. Drain. Strain sauce, return to saucepan, add orange zest and lemon juice, and cook 1 to 2 minutes, or until thick. Keep sauce warm until ready to serve.

Place duck quarters in shallow roasting pan and reheat at 450° for 30 minutes for crisp skin, or 45 minutes for extra crisp skin. Ducks have a lot of fat, so they are hard to overcook. Serve with warm sauce.

Oyster Pie

This recipe came from Tootie Williams (John W.) of Columbia. He was one of Alex's closest friends and THE BEST cook we have ever known.

Serves 8

4 Tablespoons butter
2 sleeves saltine crackers, coarsely crushed in
  sleeve
2 pints oysters
1 ½ teaspoons salt (less if the oysters are salty)
1 teaspoon black pepper
2 cups milk
1 Tablespoon dry sherry
1 Tablespoon Worcestershire sauce
¼ teaspoon sugar (if the oysters are not sweet)
2 cups cleaned and quartered medium-size
  mushrooms (about 5 ounces)

1 Tablespoon butter, room temperature
8 x 12 (2-quart) glass baking dish
12-inch frying pan

Preheat oven to 350°. Grease dish with the Tablespoon of butter.

Melt butter in frying pan on medium. Add saltines and toss 5 minutes, or until saltines have soaked up butter. Drain oysters but reserve liquor. Toss oysters with salt and pepper. Mix milk, sherry, Worcestershire sauce, and reserved liquor. Add sugar if desired. Lowcountry oysters are generally small, briny, and sweet. They will not need the sugar or as much salt.

Beginning and ending with buttered saltines, layer saltines, mushrooms, and oysters. Pour milk mixture over top. Bake at 350º for 30 to 45 minutes, or until golden brown and set.

Spoonbread

This recipe came from the original Adventure Inn at Hilton Head almost thirty years ago. We make two of these at a time for 8 people. Doubling the recipe has not worked well for us, so we find it better to have one this size for each end of the table. Spoonbread is pretty, but falls quickly. It's good even when it falls.

Serves 4

1 Tablespoon butter, room temperature

2 cups milk
1/3 cup yellow cornmeal
1/2 teaspoon sugar
1/2 teaspoon salt
2 Tablespoons butter, melted
4 egg yolks, well beaten
4 egg whites

1 1/2-quart baking dish

Preheat oven to 375º. Grease dish using Tablespoon of butter.

Scald milk on medium in saucepan until hot but not boiling. Add cornmeal, reduce to low, and cook, stirring constantly, 5 minutes, or until thick. Remove from heat and whisk in sugar, salt, and melted butter. Cool 2 or 3 minutes. Add egg yolks and mix thoroughly.

Whip egg whites in electric mixer on high until soft peaks form. Fold into batter. Pour batter into dish and bake at 375º for 30 to 40 minutes, or until it has risen and is golden

brown on top. Pass immediately, serving from baking dish.

Chocolate Pie

This pie comes from Mary Bailey of Columbia. For a fancy dessert, instead of meringue use Soft Whipped Cream (p.58) and Raspberry Sauce (p.4).

Serves 8

1 prebaked 9-inch Easy Pie Crust (p.37)

FILLING
1 1/2 cups sugar
4 Tablespoons cornstarch
1 1/2 Tablespoons all-purpose flour
1/2 teaspoon salt
3 cups milk
3 squares unsweetened chocolate, chopped
3 egg yolks, lightly beaten
1 Tablespoon butter
1 teaspoon pure vanilla extract

MERINGUE
3 egg whites
Pinch cream of tartar
6 Tablespoons sugar

Preheat oven to 375º.

TO MAKE FILLING: Mix sugar, cornstarch, flour, and salt in saucepan. Gradually whisk in milk, 3/4 cup at a time. Add chocolate and stir constantly on medium 15 minutes, or until chocolate is melted, mixture comes to a boil, and thickens. Boil 1 minute, stirring constantly, and remove from heat. Slowly stir 1 cup chocolate mixture into egg yolks. Combine thoroughly. Stir back into remaining chocolate mixture. Bring to a boil and boil 1 minute, stirring. Remove from heat. Quickly stir in butter and vanilla and pour into crust.

TO MAKE MERINGUE: Whip egg whites in electric mixer on high until frothy. Add cream of tartar. Gradually add sugar and whip

until whites are shiny and form soft peaks. Spoon meringue on top of pie, filling in circles starting from the outside and covering the crust.

Bake pie at 375° for 15 minutes, or until meringue is lightly browned. Cool completely before slicing.

Wild Rice with Mushrooms
See page 54

Asparagus
See page 107

(left) Spoonbread

The Glebe Street Cat

Phil (for Philosophy) or Tom or Nuisance are just a few of his names. His mornings begin with a moveable feast provided by students with leftover food pulled from backpacks and pockets. When a party begins at the President's House he is always there. Receptions for 500 are his favorites. The Provost's House, the Philosophy and English departments are his favorite hang-outs. He has a different menu at each house. A lot of time is spent at 4 Glebe (College Apartments) which is where his original owner, Ms. Edith Tuten, lived.

Donors Celebration
The President's House

COLLEGE CHEESE WAFERS	TOASTED PECANS

PASSED HORS D'OEUVRE

FRIED OYSTERS WITH WANDO COCKTAIL SAUCE

CRAB CAKES WITH HOMEMADE TARTAR SAUCE

SLEEPING SHRIMP

SMOKED SALMON • DILL SAUCE, CAPERS, RED ONIONS, AND CHOPPED EGG • MARINATED SHRIMP WITH MUSHROOMS AND ARTICHOKE HEARTS

SAUTÉED QUAIL BREASTS • CHEESE TORTA

COLLEGE PÂTÉ WITH CORNICHONS, WHOLE GRAIN MUSTARD, AND MELBA TOAST

GRILLED TENDERLOIN

HOMEMADE HORSERADISH SAUCE

POTATOES WITH SOUR CREAM AND CAVIAR

FRESH ARTICHOKES WITH HOLLANDAISE

TURKEY WITH CORN BREAD DRESSING CAKES AND HOMEMADE MAYONNAISE

CARAMEL DIP WITH APPLES

LEMON SQUARES • SUGAR COOKIES • BROWNIES

RASPBERRY TRIFLE • CHOCOLATE-COVERED CHERRIES

CRYSTALLIZED GINGER

CHAMPAGNE, COFFEE AND TEA

STILTON CHEESE WITH PEARS AND WALNUTS

BRANDY AND PORT

Sleeping Shrimp

Townie Krawcheck (Mrs. Leonard) of Charleston gave us this recipe, and Nancy Otis (Mrs. William L.) of Columbia named it "Sleeping Shrimp." We usually pass them at parties. They are one of the most popular hors d'oeuvre we serve.

Serves 8

½ pound extra sharp cheddar cheese, grated
¾ cup Hellmann's® mayonnaise
½ cup finely chopped jumbo yellow onion
1 Tablespoon Worcestershire sauce
½ teaspoon black pepper
1 pound boiled medium shrimp (Fast Method for Boiling Shrimp, p.135)
Ritz® crackers
Paprika

Position oven shelf 6 inches from broiler. Preheat broiler.

Mix cheese, mayonnaise, onions, Worcestershire sauce, and pepper. Place a shrimp on each cracker. Top with 1 Tablespoon of cheese mixture, spreading it out to cover the shrimp and most of the cracker. Sprinkle with paprika. Place on baking sheet and broil 1½ to 2 minutes, or until hot, bubbly, and beginning to brown. For the first 5 to 10 minutes out of the oven, Sleeping Shrimp are too hot to eat.

Cheese Torta

Serves 50 as hors d'oeuvre

12 ounces feta cheese, well drained
2 sticks butter, room temperature
1 pound cream cheese, room temperature
¾ cup Pesto
½ cup minced sun-dried tomatoes
Sprig of fresh herb

9 x 5 x 3 loaf pan lined with plastic wrap, leaving enough on each side to cover top
Crackers or thinly sliced toasted French bread

Purée feta cheese in food processor. Add butter and process. Add cream cheese and process until smooth. Spread one third of cheese mixture in loaf pan and refrigerate 45 minutes, or until set. Spread pesto over cheese and refrigerate 45 minutes. Spread second third of cheese over pesto and refrigerate 45 minutes, or until set. Spread on sun-dried tomatoes. Cover with remaining third of cheese and refrigerate 45 minutes, or until set. Fold edges of plastic wrap over top and refrigerate overnight.

When ready to serve, invert torta on a platter or cheese board. Garnish with sprig of fresh herb and serve with crackers or thinly sliced toasted French bread.

Pesto

1 ¼ cups

2 cups fresh basil leaves, washed and dried
4 large cloves garlic, minced
1 cup pine nuts, toasted
⅔ cup extra-virgin olive oil
1 cup freshly grated Parmesan cheese
Salt
Black pepper

Finely chop basil, garlic, and pine nuts in food processor. Add olive oil in slow stream. Add cheese. Salt and pepper to taste.

NOTE: Pesto will keep in the refrigerator for a week if a thin layer of olive oil is poured over top to prevent discoloration. Freezes well.

College Pâté

This is Lee Godbey's recipe, but Robert

Dickson, of Robert's of Charleston, and I had a great time testing it and changing it just a little.

Hors d'oeuvre for 50

1 cup brandy
2 Tablespoons chopped fresh thyme
  (or 1 Tablespoon dried)
1/3 cup finely diced shallots
  (3 or 4 large shallots)
1 pound ground pork from loin or butt
1 pound ground veal from top round, breast,
  or leg
1/2 pound chicken livers, drained and puréed
  down to 1/2 cup
1/4 pound bacon, finely diced
2 Tablespoons chopped fresh parsley
2 Tablespoons finely chopped black olives
2 teaspoons salt
1 teaspoon cracked black pepper
3 eggs, lightly beaten
1/2 cup heavy whipping cream

Two (9 x 5 x 3) loaf pans
Roasting pan

Cornichons (tiny French gherkin pickles
  preserved without sugar) or thinly sliced
  radishes
Whole grain mustard
Melba Toast (p.18)

Preheat oven to 325°. Line one pan with 16-inch square of aluminum foil, lightly greased.

Place brandy, thyme, and shallots in a saucepan and bring to a boil on high. Reduce to medium and briskly simmer until brandy is reduced by half. Set aside to cool.

Combine pork, veal, chicken livers, bacon, parsley, olives, salt, and cracked pepper. Mix by hand. Whisk eggs and cream mixture. Mix egg mixture and reserved brandy mixture into meat mixture. Place the meat mixture in lined pan and fold foil over top to cover. Place in roasting pan. Fill roasting pan with hot water to halfway up sides of loaf pan. Place roasting pan in 325° oven. Bake 1 1/2 hours, or until meat thermometer registers 160°.

Remove pâté in its loaf pan from roasting pan. Unfold foil from top. Cover top with plastic wrap. Place the other loaf pan on top of pâté and plastic wrap. Place something heavy inside top pan to weigh it down–a brick or large cans of soup or vegetables will do. The weight of the top pan will compress pâté so that it will slice without crumbling. Set out for 2 hours, or until cooled, and refrigerate weighted pâté overnight.

Turn out onto a platter and remove foil. Garnish with sliced cornichons and thinly sliced radishes. Slice a few pieces 1/3-inch thick to start the slicing process for guests. Serve with additional cornichons, thinly sliced radishes, whole grain mustard, and Homemade Melba Toast.

Grilled Tenderloin

This is Alex's recipe. Grilling is the most flavorful way to cook a tenderloin.

Serves 20 for party or 8 for dinner

Whole beef tenderloin, trimmed with chain
  removed
16 ounces Kikkoman® Soy Sauce
  (no substitutes)
2 Tablespoons Worcestershire sauce
2 teaspoons salt
2 teaspoons black pepper
1 teaspoon garlic powder

Marinate tenderloin in soy sauce and Worcestershire sauce for 1 hour. Salt and pepper tenderloin and sprinkle with garlic powder. Cook over very hot charcoal, turning frequently, until tenderloin reaches desired degree of doneness (approximately 15-20 minutes for medium rare). Slice thinly.

NOTE: Have butcher trim loin and remove chain.

Oven Roasted Tenderloin

This is the way Zoe Sanders Nettles (Mrs. William) of Columbia cooks her tenderloin.

Serves 20 for party or 8 for dinner

Whole beef tenderloin, trimmed with
  chain removed
2 Tablespoons olive oil
1 teaspoon salt
1 teaspoon black pepper
2 cloves garlic, crushed

String
Iron skillet
Shallow roasting pan

Preheat oven to 425°.

Tie thin tail of tenderloin under and tie string around meat at 2-inch intervals to make it evenly shaped. Rub with 1 Tablespoon olive oil, salt, pepper, and garlic. In the skillet, sear tenderloin on high in remaining olive oil 10 minutes on each side, or until dark brown. Place in roasting pan and roast at 425° for 30 minutes, or until meat thermometer reads 130° for medium rare. Let sit 20 minutes.

Homemade Horseradish Sauce

Approximately 2 cups

1 cup Hellmann's® mayonnaise
½ cup sour cream
1 Tablespoon fresh lemon juice
3 ½ Tablespoons prepared creamed
  horseradish

Mix ingredients well and refrigerate.

Turkey

Serves 8 for dinner or 30 for a party

12-15 pound turkey
Salt
Black pepper
½ stalk celery
2 jumbo yellow onions, quartered

Preheat oven to 350°.

Wash turkey inside and out with cold water. Salt and pepper inside and out, and stuff cavity with celery and onions. Place on rack in shallow baking pan, add 2 cups water, and bake turkey, breast side up, at 350° for 20 minutes per pound, or until juices run clear, legs move easily, skin is golden brown, and meat thermometer registers 175° when placed in thickest part of the thigh. Let set 30 minutes before carving and preserve the juices for gravy or Corn Bread Dressing Cakes.

Corn Bread Dressing Cakes

This is a great accompaniment to smoked or baked turkey as an hors d'oeuvre at a party, especially during the holidays. You might want to reduce the amount of pepper to ½ teaspoon if you are serving them for dinner. We make 1-inch cakes for hors d'oeuvre and 2-inch cakes for serving with dinner.

120 (1-inch) cakes or 40 (2-inch) cakes

⅓ stick butter
3 cups medium chopped celery
3 cups medium chopped jumbo yellow onion
1 recipe Skillet Corn Bread (p.14)
¾ cup broth from baked turkey, baked chicken
  (p.138), or canned chicken broth
2 eggs, beaten
½ teaspoon salt
¾ teaspoon pepper
¼ teaspoon ground sage

12-inch frying pan with a lid
2 baking sheets

Preheat oven to 350°. Grease baking sheets.

Heat butter in frying pan on medium high. Add celery, cover, and cook 5 minutes. Add onions and toss with celery. Cover and cook 10 minutes, or until celery is tender and onions are clear. Stir several times to prevent sticking. Crumble corn bread and mix with celery and onions. Add broth, eggs, salt, pepper, and sage and mix well.

If you are serving the cakes for a party, make 1-inch rounds about ½-inch thick. Bake at 350° for 30 minutes, turning the cakes after 15 minutes to brown both sides. If you are serving the cakes with dinner, make 2-inch rounds about ½-inch thick. Bake at 350° for 35 to 40 minutes, turning the cakes after 20 minutes to brown both sides.

Dressing cakes may be served warm or at room temperature. Freeze well. Thaw and heat at 350° for 15 minutes, or until hot.

Marinated Shrimp

Diane Jordan Chastain came up with this recipe when the Archbishop of Canterbury and his wife visited Trinity Cathedral in Columbia in 1987. We serve it at most of our large parties at the College. This is also a good first course over watercress or Romaine lettuce tossed with a little of the marinade.

10 servings of 5 to 6 shrimp each for a party
    or first course

1 ½ quarts water
1 ½ teaspoons salt
1 bay leaf
2 ½ pounds medium shrimp, unpeeled

½ pound medium-size fresh mushrooms,
    washed and quartered
1 (14-ounce) can artichoke hearts, drained and
    quartered

1 (2-ounce) jar capers, drained
1 jumbo yellow onion, thinly sliced
2 lemons, thinly sliced

3-gallon pot
3-gallon glass or plastic container with lid

MARINADE
1 ½ packages Good Seasons ™
    Italian Dressing Mix
½ cup vegetable oil
6 Tablespoons apple cider vinegar
4 Tablespoons water
1 ½ teaspoons prepared creamed horseradish

TO BOIL SHRIMP: Use Fast Method for Boiling Shrimp (p.135).

TO MAKE MARINADE: Whisk together Italian Dressing mix, oil, vinegar, water, and horseradish.

TO ASSEMBLE: Layer mushrooms, artichoke hearts, capers, onions, and lemons in 3-gallon container and pour marinade over all. Refrigerate overnight, turning container upside down and shaking it at least 4 times.

An hour before serving, add shrimp and toss several times. When ready to serve, drain and arrange in a glass bowl or platter. Place skewers and a small plate for used skewers near shrimp.

Crab Cakes

8 cakes for entrées or 16 cakes as hors
    d'oeuvre.

2 cups fresh bread crumbs
½ cup Hellmann's® mayonnaise
2 Tablespoons chopped fresh parsley
2 teaspoons Worcestershire sauce
1 teaspoon dry mustard
2 teaspoons salt
½ teaspoon white pepper
2 eggs, lightly beaten
2 pounds fresh jumbo lump crab meat, gently
    picked over for shells

1 stick butter

12-inch frying pan

Combine bread crumbs, mayonnaise, parsley, Worcestershire sauce, mustard, salt, pepper, and eggs. Gently fold in crab meat. Cover and refrigerate 4 hours.

Preheat oven to 200°.

Shape crab mixture into desired size cakes. Heat half of butter in frying pan. Sauté 4 large cakes or 8 small cakes on medium 5 to 10 minutes per side, or until brown on both sides. Drain on paper towels. Pour out butter and wipe out frying pan. Add remaining butter and sauté remaining cakes. The first batch may be kept uncovered on a baking sheet in a 200° degree oven until all are cooked and ready to serve.

Serve entrée-size cakes with Crab Cake Sauce (p.141) or a wedge of lemon. Serve hors d'oeuvre-size cakes with Homemade Tartar Sauce (p.142).

Fresh Artichokes with Hollandaise

This hors d'oeuvre is great for serving at a party. Don't forget to put out an attractive plate for discarded leaves. We use Hollandaise or Homemade Mayonnaise (p.127) for dipping sauce.

Serves 12 to 15

½ gallon water
2 cloves garlic, pressed
1 Tablespoon salt
3 Tablespoons apple cider vinegar
2 medium artichokes

1¼ pounds asparagus (optional) (p.107)

3-gallon pot

Combine water, garlic, salt, and vinegar and bring to a boil. Cut off approximately one inch (or a quarter) of the leaves across top of artichokes. Trim sharp tips of remaining leaves with scissors. Pull off tough row of leaves from around stem. Cut stem off flush with bottom so that artichokes can be set up flat and level. Drop artichokes into boiling water, cover, and boil 15 to 20 minutes, or until fork easily pierces bottoms. Drain artichokes upside down in a colander and cool.

Pull out light-colored center leaves from one of the artichokes. Use hollowed artichoke as a container for sauce. Pull leaves off second artichoke and arrange around hollowed artichoke. Trim fuzzy and prickly choke off bottom, cut bottom into bite-size pieces, and place around base of hollowed artichoke. (Fresh asparagus may be alternated with artichoke leaves.)

Artichokes can be prepared ahead of time and held at room temperature. Add sauce when ready to serve.

Hollandaise

Townie Krawcheck (Mrs. Leonard) taught us this trick for Hollandaise Sauce and Béarnaise Sauce. It's easy and it works every time.

½ cup

2 egg yolks, lightly beaten
1 Tablespoon fresh lemon juice
Pinch salt
Pinch cayenne pepper
1 stick cold butter

Combine egg yolks, lemon juice, salt, and cayenne pepper in top of double boiler over, but not touching, barely simmering water. Add a third of cold butter and stir until melted. Repeat 2 times. If sauce gets too thick or appears to begin to curdle, add a teaspoon of boiling water and whisk until it comes back together. Remove from heat and pour into small bowl. Sauce can sit at room temperature for several hours. Do not refrigerate. When ready to serve, stir in 1 teaspoon boiling water.

Chocolate-Covered Cherries

Presley Vaden Hogue (Mrs. Mason) of Columbia made these cherries for our family for years. Terry Hawkins, who works for ARAMARK Corporation and does a spectacular job of decorating for parties, also knows how to make these delicious little treats, and he taught us. Good chocolate is the secret. We use Ghirardelli®.

3 dozen

1 (10-ounce) jar maraschino cherries with stems
1 stick butter, room temperature
1 teaspoon pure vanilla extract
½ pound confectioners' sugar
1 Tablespoon half-and-half
½ pound high quality semisweet chocolate bar,
  chopped

Long metal icing spatula

Drain cherries and place on paper towels for 2 hours, or until dry. Cream butter and vanilla in electric mixer. Add half of confectioners' sugar and ½ Tablespoon half-and-half. Mix until well blended. Add the remaining sugar and half-and-half. Beat until mixture will form a ball when rolled in your hand. Refrigerate 5 minutes, or until firm. Pinch off 1½ teaspoonfuls of mixture, roll into balls, and place on a baking sheet. Punch a hole in each ball with your finger. Place cherries in holes and work mixture up and around cherries to cover them.

TO TEMPER CHOCOLATE, p.60

Dip covered cherries into chocolate and use fingers to smooth chocolate up to coat the whole cherry. Place chocolate-coated cherries on a baking sheet lined with wax paper and refrigerate to harden no longer than 5 minutes. The shine returns to chocolate when it hardens.

Note: Cherries may be placed in an airtight container and stored in a cool place for 3 or 4 days.

College Cheese Wafers
See page 110

Toasted Pecans
See page 9

Fried Oysters with Wando Cocktail Sauce
See pages 13, 132

Dill Sauce
See page 142

Sautéed Quail Breasts
See page 120

Potatoes with Sour Cream and Caviar
See page 132

Homemade Mayonnaise
See page 127

Caramel Dip for Apples
See page 141

Lemon Squares
See page 71

Sugar Cookies
See page 146

Brownies
See page 68

Raspberry Trifle
See page 68

Homemade Tartar Sauce
See page 142

Dessert in the
Kathleen K. Lightsey
Garden
Randolph Hall

ORANGE MOUSSE
GINGERED FRUIT COMPOTE
SANDIES

COFFEE

Orange Mousse

Robin and John Dean of Columbia brought this recipe from Japan.

Serves 8

2⅔ cups of combined orange and juice
   (about 6 large very ripe and juicy
   top-grade navel oranges)
½ cup water
5 teaspoons unflavored gelatin
1 cup sugar
¼ cup white wine
¼ cup fresh lemon juice
1 cup heavy whipping cream

Eight (4-ounce) molds lightly sprayed with vegetable spray

TO OBTAIN A COMBINATION OF ORANGE AND JUICE FROM ORANGES:
Peel and section oranges. Squeeze juice from inner white membrane. Discard membrane. Remove seeds. Purée sections and juice in a food processor or blender until liquified.

TO MAKE MOUSSE: Combine water, gelatin, and sugar in saucepan on medium and whisk continuously 5 minutes, or until gelatin and sugar are dissolved. Remove saucepan from heat and add orange and juice, wine, and lemon juice, stirring to combine well. Cool to room temperature.

Whip cream lightly until thick but not stiff. Mix into orange mixture with whisk until well blended. Divide mixture between molds. Refrigerate 3 hours, or until firm.

Unmold mousse by circling inside mold with a knife and inverting mousse onto plate. Spoon Gingered Fruit on top of mousse and serve with Pecan Sandies (p.20) on each plate.

Gingered Fruit Compote

This recipe is from Susan Boyd (Mrs. Darnall) of Columbia. She had never made it, but it "sounded good." I find she has a "great ear" for tasty food. Gingered Fruit makes a colorful display for a party when served in a clear, pretty glass bowl with skewers on the side.

Serves 10 for dessert over Orange Mousse or
      40 to 50 for a party

PRESERVED GINGER WITH SYRUP
2 cups peeled, thinly sliced fresh ginger
1½ cups sugar
½ cup light corn syrup
½ lemon, sliced and seeded

GINGERED FRUIT
2 cups fresh orange juice
2½ cups dried cranberries
3 large bananas (or 4 medium),
   cut into ⅓-inch slices
3 pink grapefruit, peeled and cut into sections
1 fresh pineapple, peeled, cored, and cut into
   bite-size pieces
1 large navel orange, peeled and cut into
   sections

Place ginger in a saucepan, add water to cover, bring to a boil, and simmer 20 minutes. Add ½ cup sugar and stir until it returns to a boil. Remove saucepan from stove, cover, and set aside overnight.

Bring ginger to a boil, add corn syrup and lemon, and simmer uncovered 15 minutes. Remove saucepan from stove, cover, and set aside 4 hours.

Add second ½ cup sugar to ginger and stir, bring to a simmer, and simmer uncovered 30 minutes. Add remaining ½ cup sugar, stir, and bring to a boil. Remove saucepan from stove, cover, and set aside 4 hours.

Soak cranberries in orange juice 30 minutes. Drain and reserve juice.

When ready to serve, bring ginger to a boil and simmer until syrup is thick enough to coat a spoon. Purée ginger with syrup and orange juice. Strain out all ginger, but reserve juice. Gingered syrup freezes well.

TO ASSEMBLE: Layer fruit in a 2-quart glass serving bowl or compote dish as follows, drizzling each layer with some of reserved juice:

Half of the cranberries, bananas, and grapefruit. Pineapple goes in the center. Remaining bananas, grapefruit, and cranberries.

Decorate with orange sections on top and finish by drizzling remaining juice over all.

NOTE: If kept overnight, drain most of juice off and reserve to pour over fruit when served. Fruit becomes too "hot" with ginger if left in juice more than 2 hours.

Sandies
See page 20

Sailing Team Snacks
Charleston Harbor
East Battery

HOMEMADE LOAF BREAD
PIMIENTO CHEESE
SPRING ONIONS AND CELERY STICKS
TERRA CHIPS

BATTERY CHOCOLATE CHIP COOKIES

BOTTLED WATER

Homemade Loaf Bread

We made 21 loaves of bread a week at Trinity Cathedral. It was our "staff of life."

2 small loaves or 1 large

STARTER
1 teaspoon sugar
¼ cup warm water (approximately 105°)
1 envelope Fleishmann's® RapidRise™
  Active Dry Yeast
3½ cups all-purpose flour
1½ cups water (room temperature)

1-quart glass jar with lid

BREAD
4 cups bread flour
2 cups whole wheat flour
1 Tablespoon salt
2 Tablespoons sugar
1¼ cups Starter
1½ cups water (room temperature)
½ cup vegetable oil

1 Tablespoon butter, melted, for greasing
  pan(s) and bread

5-quart bowl and dough hook for electric
  mixer
12-inch mixing bowl
Two (9 x 5 x 3) bread pans

TO MAKE STARTER: Combine sugar, warm water, and yeast in jar. If yeast is good, it will bubble after 10-15 minutes. Start over with new, later-dated yeast if mixture doesn't bubble. Add flour and water and stir with wooden spoon until well mixed. Leave at room temperature 2 hours. Refrigerate 48 hours before using. "Feed" starter with new batches of dough. Can be kept for 3 to 4 weeks in refrigerator.

TO MAKE BREAD: Combine bread flour, whole wheat flour, salt, and sugar together by hand in 5-quart mixing bowl. Drop in starter divided in 6 parts. Using dough hook attachment, mix on low 2 minutes. Gradually add water and mix 2 minutes. Scrape sides of bowl. Gradually add vegetable oil. Increase speed to medium and mix 15 to 20 minutes, or until dough is smooth, manageable, and no longer sticky. (If dough gets caught in dough hook, stop machine, loosen dough from hook, and continue to mix.)

Remove a cup of dough from this batch, place in starter jar, and mix well with remaining starter. Return to refrigerator.

Remove dough from electric mixer bowl and form a round ball. Place ball of dough in lightly greased bowl, grease top of dough, and cover bowl tightly with plastic wrap. Set dough in warm place (80 to 90°) for 3 to 4 hours, or until dough has doubled in size.

Punch dough down to deflate and divide into two equal pieces for small loaves. Knead on lightly floured board. Using both hands, press, fold, and turn each piece of dough continuously for 5 to 10 minutes, or until dough is smooth and elastic. After kneading, form an oblong ball with each piece and place in greased pans. Cover with dish towel and allow to rise 2 to 3 hours, or until doubled in size.

Preheat oven to 350°. Grease top of bread with remaining butter. Bake at 350° for 30 to 35 minutes, or until golden brown. To test for doneness, remove bread from pan with a towel and tap on bottom. If it sounds hollow, turn out loaves onto rack and cool to room temperature before slicing or wrapping airtight for storing. If the sound is dull, return bread to oven and bake for additional 5 minutes.

NOTE: Bread can be frozen for up to 3 weeks. Defrost overnight at room temperature. Reheat at 350° for 15 minutes to restore flavor. Cool and slice.

Pimiento Cheese for Sandwiches or as a Spread

8 sandwiches or 24 party quarters

1 pound extra sharp cheddar cheese
8 ounces chopped pimiento, drained
¾ cup Hellmann's® mayonnaise
¼ teaspoon salt
½ teaspoon pepper

1 loaf thin-sliced wheat bread

Grate cheese on large side of grater or with grating blade of food processor. Combine cheese, pimiento, mayonnaise, salt, and pepper. Mix gently with large spoon to preserve the texture of cheese and pimientos.

To make pimiento cheese sandwiches, spread each sandwich with 5 Tablespoons pimiento cheese. For party servings, cut crusts off and quarter.

NOTE: Pimiento cheese is also good as a dip with celery sticks, spring onions, or crackers.

Terra Chips

Dana Sinkler, Jr., of Charleston now lives in New York and is one of the owners of a company in Brooklyn that produces these colorful and delicious chips made from vegetable roots. They can be found in grocery stores all over the country.

Battery Chocolate Chip Cookies

4 dozen

1 stick butter, room temperature
⅓ cup + 1 teaspoon white sugar
⅓ cup + 1 teaspoon light brown sugar
½ teaspoon pure vanilla extract
1 egg
1 cup plus 2 Tablespoons all-purpose flour
½ teaspoon baking soda
½ teaspoon salt
1 cup semisweet chocolate chips
½ cup chopped pecans
½ teaspoon finely chopped orange zest

12 dozen

3 sticks butter, room temperature
1 cup + 1 Tablespoon white sugar
1 cup + 1 Tablespoon light brown sugar
1 ½ teaspoons pure vanilla extract
3 eggs
3 cups + 6 Tablespoons all-purpose flour
1 ½ teaspoons baking soda
1 ½ teaspoons salt
3 cups semisweet chocolate chips
1 ½ cups chopped pecans
1 ½ teaspoons finely chopped orange zest

Cream butter, sugar, and vanilla in electric mixer. Beat in egg. Combine flour, baking soda, and salt and mix well. Gradually add to butter mixture. Blend well. Stir in chocolate chips, nuts, and orange zest. Roll dough in wax paper into 2 rolls, or 6 rolls for large recipe, and freeze for 1 hour, or until hard.

When ready to bake cookies, preheat regular oven to 350° or convection oven to 325°. Cut 1-inch slices and quarter. Place rounded side of quarters on baking sheets and bake in either oven for 8 minutes, or until golden brown. Remove cookies from baking sheets to cool. Freeze well.

Spring Graduation Speakers Luncheon

RANDOLPH HALL CRAB SOUP
WITH
MELBA TOAST

PRESERVATION SALAD

CORNISH HENS
PICKLED PEACHES
WILD RICE WITH MUSHROOMS
ASPARAGUS
COLLEGE BISCUITS

RUM PIE

WHITE WINE
ICED TEA
COFFEE

Randolph Hall Crab Soup

This is Lee Godbey's recipe. It's identical to Lowcountry She-Crab Soup without the roe, and it's one of the most popular first courses we serve.

8 (6-ounce) servings

6 Tablespoons butter
6 Tablespoons all-purpose flour
½ cup finely chopped jumbo yellow onion
½ cup finely chopped celery
1 quart water
1 Tablespoon Worcestershire sauce
2 teaspoons salt
⅛ teaspoon cayenne pepper
2 cups half-and-half
1 pound fresh lump crab meat, gently picked over for shells

3-quart saucepan

Chopped chives for garnish
Dry sherry
Melba Toast (p.18)

Heat butter on low. Whisk in flour. Cook (what is now a roux) for 5 minutes, stirring constantly. Whisk onions, celery, water, Worcestershire sauce, salt, cayenne pepper, and half-and-half into roux. Bring mixture to a boil on medium, whisking occasionally. Reduce to low and simmer 10 minutes. Can be set aside at this point. When ready to serve, gently stir in crab meat. Don't break up the lumps. Heat soup on medium until hot. Do not boil.

Garnish soup with chopped chives. Sherry can be passed at the table. We serve Homemade Melba Toast either on the plate at the side of the soup or in a bread tray.

Cornish Hens

Serves 8, one breast quarter and leg quarter each

4 (22-ounce) Cornish hens
1 recipe Corn Bread Dressing (see Corn Bread Dressing Cakes, p.92)
2 cloves garlic, crushed
½ cup lemon juice
2 Tablespoons Worcestershire sauce
1 Tablespoon Kitchen Bouquet®
Salt
White Pepper
1 cup water
2 teaspoons butter, melted

Shallow baking dish

Preheat oven to 350°.

Wash the hens. Set breast side up and debone by cutting out the top of the ribs from the inside with a sharp knife. Cut at the top of the ribs on each side of the breastbone without cutting into wishbone or breast. Start this with a knife, then gently pull out ribs with fingers. Stuff hens with dressing. Rub outside of hens with garlic.

Mix lemon juice, Worcestershire sauce, and Kitchen Bouquet® and brush hens. Sprinkle with salt and pepper. Place in baking dish with the water in the bottom. Bake hens at 350° for 30 minutes. Reduce heat to 325°. Brush with melted butter and bake 40 minutes, or until browned and a meat thermometer inserted into the thickest part of the thigh, but not touching the bone, registers 175°.

To serve, cut breast section and leg section off separately. Scoop out dressing and serve half of a hen on top of half of dressing.

Pickled Peaches

2 quarts peaches

14 ripe, firm medium peaches (about 3 pounds)
1 quart apple cider vinegar
8 cups dark brown sugar
1 teaspoon mace
2 bay leaves
1 Tablespoon whole cloves
4 sticks cinnamon

5-gallon pot

Dip peaches in boiling water for 1 minute to make easy to peel. Peel and set aside.

Mix vinegar, sugar, mace, bay leaves, cloves, and cinnamon in pot. Bring to boil on high, add peaches, and cover. Reduce to low and cook 15 minutes, or until peaches are tender all the way to pits when pierced with a fork.

Remove peaches and boil liquid 15 minutes, or until syrupy and thick enough to coat a spoon. Pour syrup over peaches. When cool enough to handle, pick out cloves and press into peaches. Refrigerate.

Asparagus

In my opinion, large asparagus generally have a milder, more mellow flavor. Fresh white asparagus are a real treat, but are hard to find.

Serves 8

2 pounds asparagus
1 ½ quarts water
1 ½ teaspoons salt
1 Tablespoon butter, melted
1 teaspoon fresh lemon juice (optional)

12-inch frying pan

Cut off tough ends of asparagus at the point where a knife cuts easily. Bring salted water to a boil in frying pan. Add asparagus and cook 4 to 5 minutes, or until a fork easily pierces the asparagus. Cooking time depends upon size of asparagus. Drain and toss with butter and lemon juice (optional).

Rum Pie

Betsy Williams (Mrs. John W.), formerly of Columbia and now a Research Librarian at the College, gave us this wonderful recipe when we were first married.

Serves 8

CRUST
2 ⅔ cups finely crushed vanilla wafers
  (about 50 vanilla wafers)
1 stick butter, melted

10-inch pie pan

FILLING
6 egg yolks
1 cup sugar
½ cup cold water
1 envelope + 1 teaspoon unflavored gelatin
1 pint heavy whipping cream
½ cup dark rum

GARNISH
Grated semisweet chocolate or chocolate curls

TO MAKE CRUST: Preheat oven to 375°.
Mix vanilla wafer crumbs and butter. Press into pie pan and bake at 375° for 10 minutes. Cool 5 minutes.

TO MAKE FILLING: Beat egg yolks in electric mixer on medium until light colored and fluffy. Gradually beat in sugar.

Sprinkle gelatin over water in saucepan to soften. Bring to a boil on low. Slowly pour gelatin into eggs, beating at low speed.

Whip the cream until stiff and fold into egg mixture. Gently fold in rum. Refrigerate until filling is stiff enough to mound in peaks. Spoon into crust, smooth top, and refrigerate 3 hours, or until set. Garnish and serve.

Melba Toast
See page 18

Preservation Salad
See page 46

Wild Rice with Mushrooms
See page 54

Shortcut Pickled Peaches
See page 142

Graduation Reception
Courtyard
The President's House
Six Glebe Street

GRADUATION PUNCH
HOMEMADE LEMONADE

CHEESE WAFERS
SHRIMP SALAD SANDWICHES
CHICKEN SALAD SANDWICHES
PIMIENTO CHEESE
WITH CRACKERS
COUNTRY HAM BISCUITS
CREAM CHEESE AND OLIVE SPREAD
WITH CELERY STICKS

STRAWBERRIES WITH AMARETTO DIP
LEMON STICKIES
BENNE SEED COOKIES
BATTERY CHOCOLATE CHIP COOKIES
BROWNIES

Graduation Punch

We first tasted this punch at St. Francis of Assisi Episcopal Church at Lake Murray. This is a very popular, cool, and refreshing punch for summertime.

Serves 50 (4-ounce) cups

2 (10-ounce) packages frozen strawberries or
  3 pints fresh sweetened with sugar to taste
2 (46-ounce) cans pineapple juice
3 small packages strawberry Kool-Aid®
1 ½ (6-ounce) cans undiluted frozen orange juice
3 cups sugar
3 quarts water
2 quarts ginger ale, chilled

1 pint fresh strawberries, washed and sliced

6 one-quart plastic freezing containers

Blend frozen or fresh berries for 15 seconds, or until mushy. Add pineapple juice, Kool-Aid®, orange juice, sugar, and water and mix well. Divide mixture between containers and freeze until 15 minutes before serving.

When ready to serve, place the frozen mixture in the punch bowl and add ginger ale. Stir, making a slush. Add sliced berries for garnish. A second batch of this punch can be made and frozen in molds or rings to replenish and cool the punch, adding ginger ale as needed.

College Cheese Wafers

3 ½ dozen

1 stick butter
1 cup (4-ounces) grated extra sharp cheddar cheese
½ teaspoon Tabasco®
1 cup all-purpose flour
½ teaspoon salt
1 cup RICE KRISPIES®
½ cup chopped pecans

Preheat oven to 350º. Line 2 baking sheets with aluminum foil.

Cream butter, cheese, and Tabasco® in electric mixer. Combine flour and salt. Add to cheese mixture and mix well. Add RICE KRISPIES® and pecans and combine well.

Pinch off pieces of dough and roll into balls about the size of a quarter. Place on baking sheets and flatten with hand to ¼-inch thickness. Bake at 350º for 12 to 15 minutes, or until very lightly browned. Remove from baking sheets while warm. Cool.

NOTE: College Cheese Wafers can be stored in an airtight container and frozen. Take out ahead of time to thaw and reheat at 350º for about 10 minutes, or until crisp and full flavor has returned.

Shrimp Salad Sandwiches

10 sandwiches or 40 party quarters

2 cups cooked shrimp
  (Fast Method for Boiling Shrimp, p.135)
4 hard-boiled eggs
1 ½ cups Hellmann's® mayonnaise
2 teaspoons fresh lemon juice
1 teaspoon salt
1 ½ teaspoons finely ground black pepper
1 ½ cups finely chopped celery (by hand)
1 Tablespoon minced onion (by hand)
1 Tablespoon Durkee Sauce® (optional)
⅛ teaspoon granulated garlic (optional)

1 loaf thin-sliced white bread

Chop shrimp by hand in medium-size pieces. Process eggs as finely as possible. Mix mayonnaise, lemon juice, eggs, salt, pepper, celery, and onions. Add Durkee Sauce® and granulated garlic if desired. Toss shrimp in last. Refrigerate 2 hours to let flavors meld.

Spread each sandwich with ½ cup shrimp salad. For party servings, cut crusts off and quarter.

Chicken Salad Sandwiches

12 sandwiches or 48 party sandwich quarters

1 recipe Chicken Salad (p.138) with the following changes:

Tear or cut chicken into ½-inch pieces. Finely chop celery. Increase salt and pepper to 1½ teaspoons each.

1 king-size loaf thin-sliced bread

Spread each sandwich with ½ cup Chicken Salad. For party servings, cut crusts off and quarter.

Cream Cheese and Olive Spread or Dip

24 party sandwich quarters or celery dip for 30 pieces of celery

8 ounces cream cheese, room temperature
4 Tablespoons Hellmann's® mayonnaise
2 Tablespoons of juice from olives
¾ cup pimiento-stuffed salad olives

1 loaf of thin-sliced white sandwich bread
or
30 pieces celery cut ½-inch wide by 2-inches long (about 4 ribs)

Process cheese, mayonnaise, and olive juice in food processor. Coarsely chop olives by hand and stir into cheese mixture. Cover and refrigerate 4 hours, or until mixture is firm enough to spread or dip. Spread sandwich with ¼ cup of spread. Cut crusts off and quarter each sandwich.

Homemade Lemonade
See page 15

Pimiento Cheese with Crackers
See page 103

Country Ham Biscuits
See page 36

Spoleto Supper
Garden Room
The President's House
Six Glebe Street

SPOLETO GRILLED LAMB CHOPS
WITH
MINT JELLY

FRIED QUAIL
WITH
APPLE PLUM CHUTNEY

SHRIMP AND ORZO
CANTALOUPE, TOMATO, CUCUMBER,
AND MINT SALAD
GREEN BEANS WITH BENNE SEEDS
HERBED BREAD STICKS

BLUEBERRY PIE
WITH
PEACHES AND SOFT WHIPPED CREAM

ICED TEA
RED AND WHITE WINE
COFFEE

Spoleto Grilled Lamb Chops

Everybody loves Alex's grilled lamb chops when we serve them at a buffet supper.

Serves 8

16 center-cut lamb chops, 1-inch thick
  (with the largest tenderloin possible)
8 ounces Kikkoman® Soy Sauce (no substitutes)
2 teaspoons tarragon or thyme
2 teaspoons salt
2 teaspoons black pepper

Marinate chops in soy sauce 30 minutes. Salt and pepper each chop and sprinkle with herbs. Cook over very hot charcoal until chops reach desired degree of doneness (approximately 4-5 minutes on each side for medium rare).
  NOTE: Serve with mint jelly.

Fried Quail

Serves 8, two quail each

Vegetable oil sufficient to be ½-inch deep in
  skillet
16 quail, preferably with breastbone removed
Salt
Black pepper
All-purpose flour

Iron skillet

Heat oil in skillet to 300°.

Cut quail in half lengthwise and liberally salt and pepper. Dredge in flour, shaking off excess. Gently drop into hot oil and brown on each side, reducing or increasing heat as necessary to maintain a temperature of 300-325°. Quail will begin to float when almost done. Drain thoroughly on paper towels. Serve either slightly warm or at room temperature.

NOTE: Use oil previously used for browning. Second-hand oil browns better!

Apple Plum Chutney

2 pints

1 ½ cups light brown sugar
½ cup white sugar
1 ½ cups apple cider vinegar
½ Tablespoon mustard seed
½ teaspoon dry mustard
2 Tablespoons peeled and minced fresh ginger
¼ teaspoon cinnamon
¼ teaspoon mace
¼ teaspoon ground cloves
1 ½ cups peeled and chopped plums (about 1 ½
  pounds)
1 ½ cups Granny Smith apples, peeled and
  chopped in ½-inch pieces (about ½ pound
  or 2 large)
1 cup jumbo yellow onion, chopped into ½-inch
  pieces
½ cup currants
½ cup yellow raisins
½ lemon, sliced and quartered

3-quart saucepan

Combine brown sugar, white sugar, vinegar, mustard seeds, dry mustard, ginger, cinnamon, mace, and cloves in saucepan. Bring to a boil on high, stirring occasionally. Stir in plums, apples, onions, currants, raisins, and lemon and return to a boil, stirring occasionally. Cover, reduce heat to very low, and simmer 30 minutes, stirring occasionally. Partially uncover saucepan and cook 30 minutes, or until liquid is thick and syrupy. Cool to room temperature. Refrigerate, tightly covered, for at least 24 hours before serving to let flavors meld. Chutney will keep for a month in refrigerator.

Shrimp and Orzo

This recipe is good served hot, cold, or at room temperature.

Serves 8

1 gallon chicken broth, fresh or canned
1 Tablespoon salt
1 pound orzo pasta
¼ cup + 1 ½ teaspoons olive oil
1 Tablespoon fresh lemon juice
2 Tablespoons apple cider vinegar
½ teaspoon pressed garlic
½ teaspoon salt
½ teaspoon black pepper
2 teaspoons dill weed
2 pounds medium shrimp (Fast Method for
  Boiling Shrimp, p.135)
1 Tablespoon chopped green onion tops
3 Tablespoons chopped parsley

3-gallon pot

Bring chicken broth and salt to a boil on high. Add pasta, return to a boil, and cook, uncovered, 8 minutes, or until pasta is *al dente*. Drain pasta and quickly run it under cold water to stop further cooking. Whisk in 1 ½ teaspoons olive oil to keep pasta from sticking together. Cover and set aside. Combine lemon juice, vinegar, garlic, salt, pepper, and 1 teaspoon dill weed. Slowly pour in remaining ¼ cup olive oil in a stream, whisking until well blended.

When ready to serve, mix pasta, shrimp, and dressing. Toss in remaining teaspoon dill weed, green onions, and parsley.

Cantaloupe, Tomato, Cucumber, and Mint Salad

Nathalie Dupree, the famous Atlanta cook, gave us this recipe. We added a little extra mint.

Serves 8

1 large cantaloupe, cut into 1-inch cubes
1 large cucumber, cut in half lengthwise and
  sliced ⅓-inch thick
1 large tomato, cut in wedges
1 head leaf lettuce, washed and dried (optional)

DRESSING
⅔ cup red wine vinegar
1 cup vegetable oil
1 teaspoon Dijon mustard
1 teaspoon sugar
½ teaspoon salt
½ teaspoon black pepper
5 Tablespoons chopped fresh mint
3 Tablespoons chopped fresh parsley
3 Tablespoons chopped fresh chives

Whisk vinegar, oil, mustard, sugar, salt, pepper, mint, parsley, and chives together. Toss with cantaloupe and cucumbers and refrigerate 2 hours.

When ready to serve, drain cantaloupe and cucumbers, reserving marinade. Toss tomato wedges in marinade. Place cantaloupe and cucumbers in center of a serving platter with tomato wedges around edge.

For individual servings, cut tomato wedges in half and toss with cantaloupe and cucumber. Make beds of lettuce on salad plates and place cantaloupe mixture on top of lettuce.

Blueberry Pie

This recipe came from Jane Avinger (Mrs. Robert L., Jr.) of Davidson, N.C. The trick is cooking only a fourth of the blueberries to hold it together, leaving whole plump berries in every bite. We use Wadmalaw Island berries to make it special.

Serves 8

1 prebaked 9-inch Easy Pie Crust (p.37)

FILLING
4 cups fresh blueberries
¾ cup sugar
½ cup + 2 Tablespoons water
2 Tablespoons cornstarch
1 Tablespoon butter
1 Tablespoon Grand Marnier® liqueur
1 Tablespoon fresh orange juice
½ teaspoon finely chopped orange zest

3-quart saucepan

4 sliced fresh peaches (optional)

Combine 1 cup blueberries, sugar, and ½ cup water in saucepan and bring to a boil. Reduce to low and simmer 10 minutes, or until blueberries are soft. Purée in food processor. Dissolve cornstarch in 2 Tablespoons water, stir into blueberry mixture, and cook on low, stirring constantly, 10 to 15 minutes, or until mixture cooks down and thickens to almost a paste. Remove saucepan from heat. Stir in butter, Grand Marnier®, orange juice, and orange zest. Cool 5 minutes. Stir in remaining 3 cups blueberries and pour into prebaked crust. Refrigerate 2 hours.

Spoon 1 heaping Tablespoon of Soft Whipped Cream (p.58) on each piece. Serve sliced peaches on the side (optional).

Green Beans with Benne Seeds
See page 54

Herbed Bread Sticks
See French Bread page 139

Avery Research Center
Gala Dinner
The Avery Institute

CHEESE WAFERS WITH BENNE SEEDS
SAUTÉED QUAIL BREASTS

PRESERVATION SALAD

COLLEGE SHRIMP
WITH
RICE
BUTTER BEANS
TOMATOES STUFFED WITH FETA CHEESE
FRENCH BREAD

LEMON CHESS PIE

ICED TEA
WHITE OR RED WINE
COFFEE

Cheese Wafers with Benne Seeds

This is Alex's mother's recipe for cheese wafers, and she always puts a pecan half on them. Mary Hollings (Mrs. Robert) of Charleston gave us the idea of covering them in benne seeds. We consider the ones with pecans "Columbia cheese wafers." Even without anything on them, they are always popular at parties.

6 dozen

4 ounces cold extra sharp cheddar cheese
1 stick cold butter
1 cup all-purpose flour
1 teaspoon salt
⅛ teaspoon cayenne pepper
⅛ teaspoon paprika

72 pecan halves (optional)
½ cup browned benne seeds* (optional)

Grate cheese and cold butter in food processor. Remove to a bowl and blend by hand. Combine flour, salt, cayenne, and paprika. Mix with butter and cheese mixture by hand. Roll dough in wax paper into 12-inch long quarter-size rolls and refrigerate 2 hours, or until cold and hard and slices easily. Can be frozen at this point.

When ready to bake, preheat oven to 350°.

Cut cold rolls into ¼-inch thick slices. Press pecan half into each slice or roll each slice in browned benne seeds. Bake at 350° for 12 to 15 minutes, or until just beginning to brown. If they get completely brown, they have a burned taste. Remove from baking sheet while still hot. Cool. Freeze well. When ready to serve, thaw and reheat at 350° for 5 to 10 minutes, or until hot.

    * To brown benne seeds, spread on baking sheet and bake at 350° for 10 minutes, or until golden brown. Watch carefully; they get too brown quickly.

Sautéed Quail Breasts

This is Robert Dickson's recipe and has become a favorite at the College.

Party serving of 2 pieces per person

8 quail breasts, bone removed
Robert's Seasoning* or Cavender's® Greek
  Seasoning
All-purpose flour
1 stick butter
¼ cup apple brandy or apple cider

Small, heavy sauté pan.

Wash and skin quail breasts and cut in half. Sprinkle with Robert's Seasoning or Cavender's®. Lightly dredge in flour, shaking off excess. Heat butter in sauté pan. When butter barely begins to turn brown, add breasts. Do not overcrowd pan. Sauté on each side 3 to 5 minutes, or until brown. Flambé with apple brandy or stir in apple cider and heat until hot. Drain thoroughly. Serve hot with skewers.

    * Robert's Seasoning can be bought in Charleston or ordered from:
        Robert's of Charleston
        182 East Bay Street
        Charleston, S.C. 29401
        (843) 577-7565

College Shrimp

Serve College Shrimp over hot white rice (p.31) and add some of the buttery juices to give the rice a good flavor.

Serves 8

3 pounds large shrimp, peeled, deveined, and
  dried

¾ cup olive oil
2 sticks butter
1 Tablespoon Cavender's® Greek Seasoning*

Two (13 x 9 x 2) oven-proof glass baking
  dishes

Preheat oven to 400°.

Divide oil and butter between baking dishes
and heat in 400° oven until butter is melted
and just beginning to turn brown.

  Divide shrimp between baking dishes and
stir until covered with oil and butter. Sprinkle
Cavender's® Seasoning over shrimp. Bake at
400° for 6 minutes, or until shrimp turn pink
and curl. Do not overcook. Stir again and
serve.

  *Granulated garlic, Robert's Seasoning, or
seasonings of your choice can be used in place
of Cavender's®.

Butter Beans

Serves 6

1 pound shelled butter beans
3 cups water
2 teaspoons salt
2 Tablespoons butter

3-quart saucepan

Rinse beans in cold water. Discard bruised or
discolored beans. Bring beans and salted
water to a boil on high. Reduce to low and simmer 20 to 30 minutes, or until tender but not
mushy. Remove from heat and stir in butter.
Transfer beans and small amount of broth to a
serving bowl and serve, using slotted spoon.
  BUTTER BEANS AND RICE: To make 8
half-cup servings, add 2 cups cooked rice
(p.31) to drained butter beans. Add enough
butter bean broth to give rice a buttery flavor.

Tomatoes Stuffed with Feta Cheese

8 servings

8 ripe but firm medium tomatoes

FILLING
1 cup chopped tomato (from inside tomato)
6 ounces cream cheese, room temperature
½ teaspoon pressed garlic
1 teaspoon dried basil
4 teaspoons finely chopped fresh parsley
½ teaspoon salt
½ teaspoon black pepper
12 ounces feta cheese, drained well

TOPPING
2 Tablespoons toasted bread crumbs
2 teaspoons finely chopped fresh parsley
1 teaspoon olive oil

Preheat oven to 350°. Spray baking sheet with
vegetable spray.

Cut 1-inch top off tomatoes. Slice a thin layer
off bottom so that tomatoes will sit flat, being
careful not to cut through to inside. Remove
pulp and seeds. Cut out firm dividing sections
and chop to make one cup. Turn tomatoes
upside down on paper towels to drain.
  Combine cream cheese, garlic, basil, parsley, salt, and pepper in food processor. Add
feta cheese and process. Filling will be grainy.
Fold in chopped tomato. Fill tomatoes with
cheese mixture, making smooth rounded tops.
Mix bread crumbs, parsley, and olive oil and
sprinkle over cheese.
  Bake at 350° for 15 minutes, or until filling
is hot.

Lemon Chess Pie

Serves 8

1 (9-inch) Easy Pie Crust, unbaked (p.37)

1 cup sugar
4 eggs
1 ½ Tablespoons all-purpose flour
1 ½ Tablespoons plain yellow cornmeal
¼ teaspoon salt
½ stick butter, melted
¼ cup milk
¼ cup fresh lemon juice
2 teaspoons finely chopped lemon zest

Serves 160

20 (9-inch) institutional pie crusts
5 eggs beaten with 5 Tablespoons water
    for egg wash*

20 cups sugar
6 dozen eggs + 8 eggs
30 Tablespoons all-purpose flour
30 Tablespoons plain yellow cornmeal
5 teaspoons salt
2 ½ pounds butter, melted
5 cups milk
5 cups fresh lemon juice
¾ cup finely chopped lemon zest

Preheat regular oven to 350° or convection oven to 325°.

Whisk sugar and eggs together by hand. Whisk in flour and cornmeal, until lumps are removed. Whisk in salt, butter, milk, lemon juice, and lemon zest. (Industrial mixer must be used for whisking large recipe.) Pour into pie crust.

    Bake in either oven 40 to 45 minutes, or until golden brown. Cool to room temperature. Refrigerate 3 hours, or until set.

    NOTE: This pie freezes beautifully, but to taste fresh it must be thawed completely and reheated in either oven 15 minutes, or until hot.

    * For large recipe, brush sides and bottom of crusts with egg wash.

Preservation Salad
See page 46

Rice
See page 31

French Bread
See page 139

Foundation Lunch
Board Room
The Sottile House

DEVILED CRAB
BUTTER BEANS AND RICE
STEWED CORN
RIDGEWAY SQUASH CASSEROLE
SUMMER TOMATO SALAD
HOMEMADE MAYONNAISE
ARTICHOKE PICKLE
COLLEGE BISCUITS

PEACH PIE

ICED TEA
COFFEE

Deviled Crab

We got our idea for making deviled crab from Mary Leize Street (Mrs. Thaddeus).

Serves 8

2 sticks butter, melted
24 saltine crackers, finely crushed
¼ teaspoon salt
¼ teaspoon black pepper
⅛ teaspoon dry mustard
2 Tablespoons Hellmann's® mayonnaise
4 Tablespoons dry sherry
2 teaspoons Worcestershire sauce
2 teaspoons fresh lemon juice
2 heaping Tablespoons chopped parsley
1 pound fresh lump crab meat, gently picked
    over for shells

8 medium-size Blue Crab shells (can be
    ordered from seafood market)

Preheat oven to 400°.

Reserve 1 Tablespoon melted butter and 1 Tablespoon cracker crumbs.

Combine remaining butter, remaining cracker crumbs, salt, pepper, mustard, mayonnaise, sherry, Worcestershire sauce, and lemon juice and toss until butter is absorbed and all is well mixed. Gently fold in parsley and crab meat.

Divide mixture between 8 crab shells. Sprinkle reserved Tablespoon of crumbs over top. Drizzle crumbs with reserved Tablespoon of butter. Bake at 400° for 20 minutes, or until hot and tops are crisp and lightly browned.

Stewed Corn

Serves 8

4 cups fresh corn (8 ears)
¼ cup water
1 teaspoon salt
⅓ stick butter

12-inch frying pan

Cut corn off cob and scrape cobs over a deep mixing bowl. Combine corn, water, salt, and butter in frying pan and bring to a simmer on medium. Simmer, stirring frequently, 10 minutes, or until corn is tender. Cooking time will be less if corn is extremely small and tender.

Ridgeway Squash Casserole

This is the recipe of Henrietta Thomas Sanders (Mrs. Alex, Sr.) from the Thomas Family Cookbook in Ridgeway.

Serves 8

2 pounds yellow squash
2 cups chopped onions
2 teaspoons salt
1 teaspoon black pepper
½ teaspoon nutmeg
2¼ cups grated sharp cheddar cheese
2 Tablespoons butter
1 cup milk
2 eggs
16 crushed saltines
½ teaspoon paprika

2-quart casserole dish

Steam squash and onions 15 minutes, or until soft. Add 2 cups cheese and other ingredients except paprika. Pour into dish. Sprinkle remaining ¼ cup cheese and paprika on top. Bake at 350° for 45 minutes, or until brown.

Summer Tomato Salad

The taste and texture of ripe tomatoes will deteriorate when they are refrigerated. Left on the countertop in a cool place, they will become bright red and more flavorful.

Serves 8

4 very large vine-ripened tomatoes
8 leaves fresh basil
8 teaspoons Homemade Mayonnaise
  or Hellmann's® mayonnaise

Slice tomatoes ⅓-inch thick. Place 3 slices on each plate. Tear basil leaves into pieces, sprinkle over tomatoes, and top with teaspoon of mayonnaise.

Homemade Mayonnaise

Virginia Holland (Mrs. Warren) of Columbia taught us to make this. *(This recipe contains uncooked eggs, which are not acceptable to many cooks.)*

1 ⅓ cups

1 egg
½ teaspoon salt
Pinch paprika
Pinch cayenne pepper
Pinch dry mustard
1 ¼ cups vegetable oil
2 Tablespoons fresh lemon juice (or to taste)

Process egg, salt, paprika, cayenne pepper, mustard, and ¼ cup of oil in food processor. With machine running, slowly pour in ½ cup of remaining oil in a thin stream. Stop processor and add lemon juice. Restart and pour in remaining ½ cup of oil in a thin stream. Add more lemon juice if desired. Refrigerate.

Artichoke Pickle

This recipe came from Betsy Williams (Mrs. John W.). She's always given us several jars for Christmas. They seldom last until Easter.

12 pints

5 pounds cabbage, outer green leaves removed
2 red peppers, cored and seeded
1 green pepper, cored and seeded

1 ½ pounds jumbo yellow onions
3 cups sugar
1 cup all-purpose flour, sifted
4 ½ Tablespoons dry mustard
3 Tablespoons turmeric
4 Tablespoons salt
2 quarts apple cider vinegar
12 cups Jerusalem artichokes, scrubbed,
  washed well, and chopped in ½-inch pieces

3-gallon pot
12 pint jars with tops, sterilized and kept hot in boiling water

Chop cabbage, peppers, and onions by hand into ½-inch pieces. Set aside in separate bowls.

Mix sugar, flour, mustard, turmeric, and salt in pot until there are no lumps. Add vinegar and stir until smooth. Bring to a boil on medium high, stirring constantly.

Reduce heat to medium and add artichokes. Bring to a simmer, stirring constantly. Add cabbage and onions. Boil gently for 20 minutes, stirring constantly. Add peppers and boil gently, stirring constantly, for 10 minutes, or until sauce thickens and vegetables are soft but not mushy. (Hot pickle will continue to cook in jars.)

Place immediately into hot, sterilized jars. Wipe rims with damp cloth and cover with hot, sterilized canning tops.

Pickle will keep for 6 months in a refrigerator.

Peach Pie

Bridget Hindman (Mrs. Russell), Special Events and Faculty House Coordinator at the College, gave us this recipe.

Serves 8

2 rounds of Easy Pie Crust dough (p.37)
9-inch pie pan

FILLING
1 egg
¾ cup sugar
¼ cup all-purpose flour
¼ teaspoon mace
1 Tablespoon fresh lemon juice
½ teaspoon pure almond extract
6 cups peeled and sliced fresh peaches

Preheat oven to 400°.

Lightly beat egg, sugar, flour, mace, lemon juice, and almond extract. Add peaches and toss. Pour into bottom crust and top as directed (p.37). Bake at 400° for 15 minutes. Reduce heat to 350° and bake 45 minutes, or until crust is golden brown. Cool 2 to 3 hours before slicing. Pie can be stored at room temperature for 24 hours in a cool place.

Butter Beans and Rice
See page 121

College Biscuits
See page 3

Additional Recipes

HORS D'OEUVRE
APPETIZERS
SALADS
SOUPS
SEAFOOD
POULTRY
BREADS AND PASTRY
CONDIMENTS AND SAUCES
RICE, POTATOES, GRITS, AND PASTA
VEGETABLES
BEVERAGES
DESSERTS

HORS d'OEUVRE

Fried Oysters

Serves 6 to 8 as hors d'oeuvre

*Vegetable oil sufficient to be ½-inch deep in
    skillet
1 pint select oysters
Salt
Black pepper
All-purpose flour
Cornmeal
White pepper*

Iron skillet
Skewers
Homemade Tartar Sauce (p.142) or Wando
    Cocktail Sauce (p.13)

Heat oil in skillet to 350°.

Drain and liberally salt and pepper oysters.
Dredge in a mixture of half flour and half
cornmeal. Gently drop into hot oil and fry 2 to
3 minutes, or until brown. Oysters will float to
top when done. Drain thoroughly on paper
towels. Sprinkle with salt and white pepper to
taste. Pass immediately with skewers,
Homemade Tartar Sauce, and/or Wando
Cocktail Sauce.

    NOTE: Use oil previously used for brown-
ing. Second-hand oil browns better!

Potatoes with Sour Cream and Caviar

This is a wonderful accompaniment to beef
tenderloin or roast beef at a party.

32 halves as hors d'oeuvre

*16 small new potatoes (about 2 pounds)
1 Tablespoon salt
1 ½ quarts water*

*1 ½ cups sour cream
2 ounces red caviar*

3-quart saucepan

Wash potatoes, being careful not to tear skin.
Cover potatoes with salted water and bring to
a boil on high. Reduce to medium, partially
uncover, and boil 20 minutes, or until a fork
easily pierces potatoes. Drain. Cool to room
temperature and cut in half. Cut thin slice off
bottom of each half so potatoes will sit flat.
Scoop out ½ teaspoon of potato from center of
each half. Spoon a teaspoon of sour cream into
each center. Potatoes and sour cream can sit in
a cool place for 3 to 4 hours. Before serving put
⅛ teaspoon of caviar on top of sour cream.

APPETIZERS

Cantaloupe and Prosciutto

Good melon draped with prosciutto makes an
excellent first course on a summer night. We
also add a slice of melon with prosciutto
wrapped around the center as an accompaniment to shrimp salad and chicken salad plates.
A fully ripe, flavorful melon is the key to success.

Serves 6 as an appetizer

*1 large cantaloupe
12 paper-thin slices prosciutto
Freshly cracked black pepper
1 lime*

Place 3 slices cantaloupe on each of 6 plates.
Drape 2 slices prosciutto over melon, sprinkle
with cracked pepper, and serve with wedge of
lime.

SALADS

Cranberry Salad

Barbara Streett (Mrs. Richard M., Sr.) gave us this recipe when we were cooking at Trinity Cathedral. It's always a favorite during the holidays.

Serves 10

1 cup water
1 (3-ounce) package cherry Jell-O®
½ cup sugar
1 (8-ounce) can crushed pineapple
1 Tablespoon fresh lemon juice
1 small orange
1 cup ground fresh cranberries (grind in food processor)
1 cup hand-chopped celery
½ cup hand-chopped pecans
1 head leaf lettuce, washed and dried
Hellmann's® mayonnaise

Ten (4-ounce) muffin pans or salad molds, lightly oiled

Serves 150

15 cups water
7 (6-ounce) and 1 (3-ounce) packages cherry Jell-O®
7½ cups sugar
1 (#10) can crushed pineapple
1 cup fresh lemon juice
15 small oranges
15 cups ground fresh cranberries (grind in food processor)
15 cups chopped celery
7½ cups chopped pecans
15 heads leaf lettuce, washed and dried
Hellmann's® mayonnaise

Three (11 x 19 x 2½) pans or
    150 (4-ounce) molds, lightly oiled

Boil water and stir in Jell-O® and sugar until dissolved. Drain pineapple and reserve juice. Add lemon juice to pineapple juice and enough water to make ½ cup of liquid (7½ cups of liquid for the large recipe). Combine with Jell-O® mixture. Wash orange and slice. Do not peel. Remove seeds. Grind orange in food processor. Add pineapple, orange, cranberries, celery, and pecans to Jell-O® mixture. Combine well. Pour into muffin pans or salad molds and refrigerate until congealed.

TO ASSEMBLE: Make bed of lettuce on salad plates and turn out salads onto lettuce. Garnish with dollop of mayonnaise.

Tomato Aspic

Use your favorite Bloody Mary mix to make aspic. We use Mr and Mrs T®. If serving as a first course when the entrée is not seafood, add 3 boiled shrimp to each salad as a garnish.

Serves 8

ASPIC
2 packages unflavored gelatin
1 quart Bloody Mary mix

8 (4-ounce) molds lightly sprayed with vegetable spray

DRESSING
1 cup cottage cheese
½ cup Hellmann's® mayonnaise
2 Tablespoons fresh lemon juice
2 Tablespoons finely chopped green pepper
2 Tablespoons toasted pecan pieces
½ teaspoon salt

ACCOMPANIMENTS
1 (14-ounce) can artichoke hearts, drained and quartered
1 (14-ounce) can hearts of palm, drained and sliced
2 avocados, peeled and sliced in eighths

24 shrimp, boiled, peeled, and deveined
  (optional), Court-Bouillon Method for Boiled
  Shrimp, (p.135)
1 head leaf lettuce, washed and dried

TO MAKE ASPIC: Dissolve gelatin in 1 cup Bloody Mary mix. Bring remaining 3 cups mix to a boil. Immediately remove from heat. Stir gelatin into hot liquid until dissolved. Do not put it back on heat as boiling will make aspic tough. Divide mixture between molds. Refrigerate 4 hours, or until congealed.

TO MAKE DRESSING: Combine cottage cheese, mayonnaise, lemon juice, peppers, pecans, and salt. Stir to mix well. Refrigerate until ready to use.

TO ASSEMBLE: Make bed of lettuce on salad plates. Invert aspic onto lettuce. Spoon dressing equally around base of each aspic. Arrange artichokes, hearts of palm, and avocado around dressing. If using shrimp, arrange over aspic.

SOUPS

Broccoli Soup

This is one of many soups Raven Graydon Tarpley (Mrs. Peter) taught us to make at Trinity Cathedral.

8 (9-ounce) servings

2 heads fresh broccoli (about 2 pounds)
5 ½ cups chicken broth, fresh or canned
1 ½ cups minced celery
1 ½ cups chopped onion
6 Tablespoons butter
6 Tablespoons all-purpose flour
3 cups half-and-half
1 teaspoon marjoram
1 teaspoon thyme
1 teaspoon salt
1 teaspoon white pepper

Cook broccoli (p.143) in chicken broth, substi-tuting broth for water and omitting baking soda and salt. Drain broccoli, but reserve broth.

Sauté celery and onions in butter on medium 10 minutes, or until soft. Whisk in flour and cook 2 minutes, whisking constantly. Slowly whisk in reserved chicken broth. Scald half-and-half on medium until hot but not boiling. Process broccoli in food processor and combine with chicken broth mixture. Add half-and-half, marjoram, thyme, salt, and pepper. Cook on low heat, whisking occasionally, until hot and thickened. Do not boil or it will curdle and separate.

Craig Cafeteria Clam Chowder

This is a less expensive seafood chowder than Oyster Stew or Randolph Hall Crab Soup. With a sandwich, it makes a great lunch on a cool day.

Serves 8

1 (10¾-ounce) can Campbell's®
  Cream of Celery Soup
1 (10¾-ounce) can Campbell's®
  Cream of Potato Soup
2 (6½-ounce) cans chopped clams and juice
2⅔ cups milk
½ stick butter
Worcestershire sauce to taste
White pepper to taste

3-quart pot
Oyster crackers

Serves 100

3 (50-ounce) cans Campbell's®
  Cream of Celery Soup
3 (50-ounce) cans Campbell's®
  Cream of Potato Soup
2 (51-ounce) cans chopped clams and juice
2½ gallons milk

2 ½ pounds butter
Worcestershire sauce to taste
White pepper to taste

Two (3-gallon) pots
Oyster crackers

Combine ingredients in pot (for larger recipe, divide ingredients between pots) and whisk together. Heat on low until hot. Do not boil. Serve with oyster crackers.

SEAFOOD

Boiled Shrimp - Two Methods

If shrimp are going to be used in a flavored dish such as Marinated Shrimp or Shrimp Salad, use the "Fast Method" for boiling. If serving plain, with lemons and cocktail sauce, it's worth the time to use the "Court-Bouillon Method."

8 servings, or about 8 shrimp per person

FAST METHOD FOR BOILING SHRIMP
1 ½ quarts water
1 ½ teaspoons salt
1 bay leaf
2 pounds medium shrimp, unpeeled

3-gallon pot

Bring salted water and bay leaf to a boil on high. Add shrimp and return to full boil. Boil 2 to 3 minutes, or until shrimp curl and turn pink. Drain shrimp in colander, sprinkle lightly and quickly with cold water, and spread on baking sheet to stop further cooking. Peel when cool enough to handle.

COURT-BOUILLON METHOD FOR BOILED SHRIMP
3 quarts water

1 Tablespoon salt
1 teaspoon black peppercorns
½ lemon, thinly sliced
1 large garlic clove
2 ribs celery
2 bay leaves
2 pounds medium shrimp, unpeeled

3-gallon pot

Bring salted water, peppercorns, lemon, garlic, celery leaves, and bay leaves to a boil on high. Reduce to low and simmer 30 minutes to develop flavor. Increase heat to high and bring water to a full boil. Add shrimp and return to full boil. Boil 2 to 3 minutes, or until shrimp curl and turn pink. Drain, sprinkle with cold water, spread on baking sheet, and peel as directed in Fast Method.

TIPS FOR BOILING SHRIMP:

1) To make sure shrimp are covered with water and pot is large enough, pre-measure with cold water before cooking.

2) Cook shrimp with shells on to preserve flavor.

3) Smaller shrimp will take less time to cook. See Boiled Creek Shrimp (p.8). In comparison, "medium" shrimp are fairly large.

4) Using cold water to cool hot shrimp takes away flavor. Use as little as possible.

5) Peel shrimp when cool enough to handle. Warm shrimp peel easier than cold shrimp.

Sautéed Flounder

Robert Dickson, the famous restaurateur of Robert's of Charleston, has been my friend and food consultant for over twenty-five years. This is his recipe.

Serves 8

FLOUNDER
2 pounds flounder fillets, skinned
2 cups all-purpose flour
1 teaspoon salt
½ teaspoon black pepper
3 eggs, lightly beaten
2 cups toasted bread crumbs
3 sticks butter
4 Tablespoons olive oil

SAUCE
½ cup diced shallots (about 3 large)
1 cup dry white wine (vermouth is best)
8 Tablespoons fresh lemon juice
5 Tablespoons chopped parsley
Lemon wedges
Parsley sprigs

12-inch frying pan

Preheat oven to 200°.

Combine flour, salt, and pepper. Dip both sides of fillets into seasoned flour, then into beaten eggs, and finally into bread crumbs. Heat ⅓ stick butter and 1 Tablespoon olive oil in frying pan until foaming. Place 4 breaded fillets in pan and sauté 3 minutes on each side. The thickness of the fish determines length of time it takes to cook. It's done when it's opaque; cut at its thickest part to check. Transfer to baking sheet and place in 200° oven until all are done and sauce is ready.

Deglaze pan with small portion of white wine. This method ensures that pan remains clean for next batch of fillets. This wine, once heated, becomes the liquid for sauce. Each time you finish sautéing fillets, deglaze pan and pour wine into clean bowl. At end of sautéing, deglaze pan for the last time and return all wine back to pan to begin making sauce. Reduce wine by half on high. Add shallots and lemon juice. Cook 3 minutes. Turn off heat and quickly whisk in remaining butter to give a creamy consistency to the sauce. Add

parsley. Using a spatula, transfer filets to warm plates or platter. Garnish with lemon wedges and parsley sprigs and pour sauce over fillets.

NOTE: An alternative method for sautéing a large amount of fish is to sauté each fillet only enough to brown each side and place fillets on a greased baking sheet. Finish cooking fillets on baking sheet at 350° for 10 minutes. This process is also used when preparing ahead for a large party. Fillets can sit at room temperature for about 1 hour before serving.

Shrimp Creole

We recommend one cup of creole and one cup of rice per person in this recipe. If this is a one-dish meal for hearty eaters, one-and-a-half times this recipe will give you plenty.

Serves 8

¼ pound bacon
3 jumbo yellow onions, chopped
2 green peppers, chopped
5 (14.5-ounce) cans whole tomatoes
2 teaspoons sugar
2 bay leaves
1 ½ cups hand-torn fresh white bread crumbs (2 slices bread)
1 ½ teaspoons salt
1 teaspoon black pepper
2 teaspoons Worcestershire sauce
2 ½ pounds (50- to 60-count) boiled shrimp (Fast Method for Boiling Shrimp, p.135)

3-gallon pot

Serves 50

1 ½ pounds bacon
18 jumbo yellow onions, chopped
12 green peppers, chopped
1 case (#10 cans) whole tomatoes
4 Tablespoons sugar
12 bay leaves
9 cups hand-torn fresh white bread crumbs

3 Tablespoons salt
2 Tablespoons black pepper
4 Tablespoons Worcestershire sauce
15 pounds (50- to 60-count) boiled shrimp
 (Fast Method for Boiling Shrimp, p.135)

Two (5-gallon) pots
Fry bacon until crisp. Remove bacon, crumble, and reserve. Add onions and peppers to bacon fat and sauté on medium 15 minutes (30 minutes for large recipe), or until soft. Process or mash tomatoes with their juice until they are in small pieces and add to onions and peppers. Add sugar, bay leaves, bread crumbs, reserved bacon, Worcestershire sauce, salt, and pepper. Simmer on low, partially covered, 2 hours (4 hours for large recipe), or until cooked down to a smooth, thick sauce. Add shrimp and serve over rice (p.31) or transfer to a cool container, partially cover, and refrigerate. Freezes well.

Shrimp Salad

6 cups or 8 shrimp salad plates with ¾ cup
 shrimp salad each

SHRIMP SALAD
4 hard-boiled eggs
1 ½ cups Hellmann's® mayonnaise
1 Tablespoon fresh lemon juice
½ teaspoon salt
1 ½ teaspoons finely ground black pepper
2 cups medium chopped celery (by hand)
1 Tablespoon minced onion (by hand)
1 Tablespoon Durkee Sauce® (optional)
2 pounds boiled medium shrimp (Fast Method
 for Boiling Shrimp, p.135)

ACCOMPANIMENTS
8 small vine-ripened tomatoes
1 head leaf lettuce, washed and dried
2 avocados, peeled and sliced in eighths
8 slices cantaloupe wrapped in prosciutto
 (p.132)
24 chilled cooked asparagus (p.107)

8 small bunches grapes
8 strawberries

TO MAKE SHRIMP SALAD: Process eggs as finely as possible in food processor. Mix mayonnaise, lemon juice, eggs, salt, pepper, celery, onion, and optional Durkee Sauce® in a large bowl. Toss shrimp in last. Cover and refrigerate 2 hours to let flavors meld.

TO ASSEMBLE: Use method for Chicken Salad Plate (p.139).

Steamed Oysters
Some Musings on the Oyster

In the broad expanses of Spartina marsh that lie between the barrier islands and the mainland south of Awendaw are numerous small hummocks that were the scenes of oyster roasts of South Carolina's first citizens, the Sewee Indians. Large piles of scorched shells and broken pieces of decorated pottery provide mute testimony to the longevity of one of South Carolina's most enduring gustatory traditions, the oyster roast.

In the not-too-distant past, oyster roasts were actually roasts. Huge stocks of split oak were brought to the scene, pits dug, fires built, and large sheets of steel were set over the fire. Bushel bags of oysters were dumped onto the hot metal plates and covered with wet gunnysacks. The sacks contained the heat and the steam and were kept dampened lest they catch on fire.

At the appropriate moment the steaming pile was uncovered and brought to the table a shovelful at a time. On the table were catsup and horseradish cocktail sauces, hot pepper vinegar, piles of rags or gloves for holding the hot oysters, and implements for extracting the little beasts from their shells and delivering them to awaiting palates.

Ancient methodology has succumbed to technology and now most oysters are steamed in various and sundry large retorts in much larger amounts than were earlier possible. The

137

debate on whether truly roasted oysters taste better than steamed ones varies in intensity according to who is having to perform the labor.

The rhetoric notwithstanding, an oyster roast by any means is always a crowd pleaser and follows the theory of entertainment that if you are standing up and eating with your fingers, you've got to be having fun.

The rule of thumb on procuring oysters is roughly 7 people per S.C. bushel or 5 people per 40 lb. box. These quantities will vary according to what else is being served and the method being used to cook them. Quantities may also vary according to the number of tables used; this applies particularly in reference to larger crowds.

There are many commercially prepared cocktail sauces for dipping the shucked oyster into. One good homemade receipt is 1 (40 oz.) bottle Heinz catsup, 1 (5 oz.) jar KRAFT® PREPARED Horseradish (not horseradish sauce), 2 Tablespoons wooster, 1 Tablespoon black pepper, and 1½ cups apple cider vinegar. It is preferred to have the sauce a little loose so as to cover the oyster better. There are some places that use hot pepper vinegar, also known as "disinfectant," to dip their oysters in.

Generous amounts of saltine crackers and paper towels should be provided on the tables.

It may be interesting to note that oysters belong to the family Ostreidae of which there are three genera: Ostrea, Crassostrea, and Pycnodonte. Our principal edible oyster in South Carolina and the Gulf Coast is the species Crassostrea virginica.

Linnaeus himself waxed poetic about the oyster in his 1758 text *Systema Naturae*, where he wrote, "Ostrea. Animal Tethys, testa bivalvis inaequivalvis, subdurita. Cardo edentulous and tossula cava ovata, striisque lateralibus transversis. Vulva anusve nullus."

Unbelievable, isn't it?!

In closing, it would be appropriate to say that the presence of oysters demands the provision of ample quantities of "appropriate libations" such as cold beer and crisp white wine, or, as the British do – champagne.

It has been seen time and time again that a guest who has just consumed a succulent oyster followed by a sip of cold beer will spontaneously bow his head in a moment of silent prayer. Amen.

Ben McC. Moise
Game Warden

(Written by flashlight in the predawn hours of a chilly December morning on a Santee River rice field dike, waiting for trespassers to come out of the field.)

POULTRY

Chicken Salad

Hot Sour Cream Muffins (p.140) are delicious with both Chicken Salad and Shrimp Salad plates.

6 cups or 8 salad plates with ¾ cup chicken salad each

BAKED CHICKEN
2 (approximately 3-pound) chickens
Salt
Black pepper
8 ribs celery
1 jumbo yellow onion

CHICKEN SALAD
6 hard-boiled eggs
1⅓ cups Hellmann's® mayonnaise
1 teaspoon fresh lemon juice
1¼ teaspoons salt
1¼ teaspoons black pepper
2 cups medium chopped celery

ACCOMPANIMENTS
1 head leaf lettuce, washed and dried
8 small vine-ripened tomatoes
2 avocados, peeled and sliced in eighths

8 slices cantaloupe wrapped in prosciutto
   (p.132)
24 cold cooked asparagus (p.107)
8 small bunches grapes
8 strawberries

TO BAKE CHICKEN: Preheat oven to 350°.

Wash chickens inside and out with cold water. Salt and pepper chickens inside and out. Stuff each cavity with 4 ribs celery and ½ onion. Place chickens on rack in shallow baking pan. Add 2 cups water. Bake chickens, breast side up, at 350° for approximately 20 minutes per pound, or until juices run clear and legs can be easily moved. Skins should be golden brown, and a meat thermometer should register 180°. Remove chickens from pan and cool at room temperature until cool enough to handle. Reserve pan juices and drippings if needed for another recipe.

TO MAKE CHICKEN SALAD: Pull meat off chickens in approximately 1-inch pieces but use all meat no matter how small. Process eggs as finely as possible. Mix eggs, mayonnaise, lemon juice, salt, pepper, and celery in large bowl. Gently toss chicken in mayonnaise mixture. Cover and refrigerate for 3 hours before serving.

TO ASSEMBLE: Make bed of lettuce on 8 plates. Cut tomatoes in 6 wedges almost to bottom. Set tomatoes in center of lettuce and fan wedges out. Place ¾ cup of chicken salad in middle of each tomato. Arrange avocados, melons, asparagus, grapes, and strawberries around tomatoes.

College Chicken Bog

Along with salad, bread, and a dessert, this makes a very filling meal that can easily be doubled or tripled for a large hungry crowd.

Serves 8 to 10

2 gallons water
3 Tablespoons salt
2 (3 ½-4 pound) chickens

16 slices bacon (about 1 pound)
4 cups chopped jumbo yellow onion
4 cups Uncle Ben's Converted® White Rice
1 teaspoon black pepper

3-gallon iron or heavy pot with tightly
   fitting lid

Bring water and 2 Tablespoons salt to a boil. Add chickens, return to a boil, and gently boil on medium high for 1 hour, or until legs of chickens can be easily moved. Remove chickens and set aside. Strain broth and skim fat off top.

Fry bacon until crisp in same pot. Remove bacon and reserve. Add onions to bacon fat and cook 15 minutes, or until soft and beginning to brown. Add rice, 2 teaspoons of salt, and 2 quarts of chicken broth. Cover tightly and bring to a boil on high. Reduce heat to low and cook 30 to 40 minutes, or until all liquid has been absorbed.

Pull meat off chickens in approximately 2-inch pieces, but use all meat no matter how small.

Crumble bacon. When rice is done, add chicken, bacon, and the remaining teaspoons of salt and pepper. Toss until hot. Serve immediately, or dish will have to be seasoned again.

NOTE: If you have two (10-inch) iron skillets, divide recipe between them after you have boiled chickens. A brown crust will form on the bottom and is delicious when tossed with chicken and bacon.

BREADS AND PASTRY

French Bread

This recipe came from Betsy Williams (Mrs. John W.). Betsy has been making delicious bread for years. She says that French bread should not be kneaded like loaf bread. I like to knead bread and make it all in one day. Betsy lets the dough rise in the refrigerator overnight on the second rise and she uses all-purpose flour. I changed her recipe a little. It's good both ways!

2 loaves

4 cups bread flour
2 teaspoons salt
1 ½ cups warm tap water (approximately 105°)
1 Tablespoon sugar
1 envelope Fleishmann's® RapidRise™ Active
  Dry Yeast
1 Tablespoon olive oil or melted butter

3-quart mixing bowl
2 French bread pans or homemade pans
  shaped by doubling heavy-duty
  aluminum foil and placing on a baking
  sheet, lightly greased with butter or olive
  oil

Combine flour and salt in mixing bowl.

Mix the water, sugar, and yeast in a measuring cup. After 15 minutes, the mixture should bubble and foam. Make a well in the flour and add yeast mixture, stirring from the center out until the mixture begins to form a ball of dough. Pat ball into shape with hands. Leave dough in bowl. Lightly brush with olive oil or butter. Cover bowl tightly with plastic wrap. Place dough in a warm place (80-90°) for approximately 1 hour, or until dough has doubled in size.

Punch down dough to deflate, cover bowl again, and let sit for approximately 1 hour, or until it doubles in size again. Punch down. Knead dough on a lightly floured board. Using both hands, press, fold, and turn dough continuously for 2 to 3 minutes.

Roll dough into 2 loaves, pinching edges and ends together so that dough doesn't pop open when it starts to rise again. Roll until edges are smooth. Place in pans. Cover with dish towel and put in warm place to rise for about 1 hour, or until doubled in size.

Preheat oven to 400°. Bake 20 to 25 minutes, or until golden brown. Brush with olive oil or butter the last 5 minutes of baking. To test for doneness, remove one loaf carefully from pan with towel and tap bottom. If it sounds hollow, turn loaves onto rack and cool completely before slicing or wrapping airtight for storing. If sound is dull, return to oven and bake another 5 minutes.

* For hard crust, spray or brush bread with cold water before putting into oven. Bake for 10 minutes, reduce heat to 325°, and spray or brush again with cold water. Bake 35 minutes, or until golden brown.

NOTE: This recipe makes 24 bread sticks. Shape into ½-inch "sticks" that are 6 inches long and half as thick as you want the finished sticks to be. Place bread sticks on greased baking sheet, cover with dish towel, and put in warm place to rise for 1 hour, or until doubled in size. Before baking, brush with* 1 egg beaten with 1 tablespoon water and sprinkle with granulated garlic, dried parsley, or dried marjoram. Bake at 400° for 10 to 12 minutes, or golden brown.

Sour Cream Muffins

Perfect with a chicken salad or shrimp salad plate.

36 mini-muffins

2 sticks butter, room temperature
2 cups sour cream
2 cups self-rising flour

3 mini-muffin tins

Preheat oven to 350°.

Mix butter and sour cream in electric mixer on low until well blended. Fold in flour by hand. Spoon 1 Tablespoon batter into each muffin cup. Bake at 350° for 25 minutes, or until golden brown. Serve or set aside on paper towels until ready to serve. Reheat at 350° until hot.

Toasted Saltines

1 sleeve saltines
1 stick butter

12-inch frying pan

Preheat oven to 300°.

Melt butter in frying pan. Place saltines in melted butter. Turn over to coat both sides and place on baking sheet. Bake at 300° for 10 minutes. Turn and continue to bake 5 minutes, or until golden. Cool.

CONDIMENTS AND SAUCES

Caramel Dip for Apples

Marion Sullivan has been a Food Consultant in Columbia, Hilton Head, and now Charleston. She has added her special touch to this book and to the food at the College. This is just one of the recipes from her collection.

3 cups

3 cups sugar
½ cup water
½ teaspoon fresh lemon juice
2 cups heavy whipping cream
6 Tablespoons cold unsalted butter, cut into 6 pieces and kept in refrigerator
½ teaspoon pure vanilla extract
⅛ teaspoon cinnamon
⅛ teaspoon mace

3 Granny Smith apples
3 Red Delicious apples
2 cups orange juice

5-quart pot
Pastry brush

Combine sugar, water, and lemon juice in pot. Heat on low, stirring gently until sugar dissolves. Using a clean pastry brush, wash down sides of pot with water several times to dissolve any grains of sugar.

Heat cream in separate saucepan until hot but not boiling.

When sugar has dissolved, increase heat to medium. Do not stir any more after this point. As water evaporates, sugar will get thicker and have larger bubbles. Watch carefully. The sugar will begin to color and in approximately 10 minutes will very quickly go from light golden to deep golden. Caramel will taste burned if sugar gets too brown. When sugar is deep golden, remove pot from heat and slowly pour in hot cream a little at a time. The mixture will bubble violently. As soon as cream is incorporated, stir in cold butter. Mixture will cool down. Stir in vanilla. Sprinkle in cinnamon and mace, stirring to prevent lumping. Cool to room temperature and serve or refrigerate up to 2 weeks. Freezes well. Heat when ready to use.

When ready to serve, slice 2 of each kind of apple and put slices in orange juice to prevent browning. Heat Caramel Dip, pour into small chafing dish or fondue dish, place on tray, and fan slices around for dipping. Garnish tray with remaining apples.

Crab Cake Sauce

This is a very light sauce to serve with Crab Cakes (p.93) when serving for a first course or an entrée. At the College, we spoon this sauce on the plate under the crab cakes instead of on top. It's prettier that way.

2 cups

½ stick butter
¼ cup all-purpose flour
1 ¼ cups milk
½ cup white wine (we recommend a Chardonnay)

½ teaspoon salt
¼ teaspoon white pepper
2 teaspoons peeled and grated fresh horseradish
2 Tablespoons finely chopped fresh lemon zest
   (about 2 lemons)

8-inch saucepan

Melt butter in saucepan on low. Blend in flour and cook, whisking constantly, 2 to 3 minutes, or until mixture thickens and becomes foamy. Remove from heat. When butter and flour stop foaming, whisk in milk. Return to heat and cook 4 to 5 minutes on low, or until thick. Whisk in wine, salt, pepper, horseradish, and lemon zest and cook 1 minute. Set aside until ready to serve. Reheat on low 3 minutes, or until hot.

Dill Sauce

2 cups

1 pound cream cheese, room temperature
½ cup sour cream
½ cup Homemade Mayonnaise (p.127)
1 Tablespoon fresh lemon juice
2 green onions, finely chopped
8 Tablespoons chopped fresh dill

Process cream cheese until smooth. Add sour cream, mayonnaise, and lemon juice and process until smooth. Stir in onions and dill. Refrigerate 3 hours.

Homemade Tartar Sauce

Townie Krawcheck (Mrs. Leonard) gave us this recipe.

1½ cups

1 cup Homemade Mayonnaise (p.127)
¼ cup chopped green onions, including tops
2 Tablespoons sweet relish
1 Tablespoon chopped pimiento

1 Tablespoon finely chopped capers
½ Tablespoon fresh lemon juice
1 teaspoon Dijon mustard
½ teaspoon salt
½ teaspoon black pepper

Combine ingredients. Refrigerate 3 hours to allow flavors to meld.

Shortcut Pickled Peaches

Dot Gilbert (Mrs. Claude) of Columbia taught us this trick at Trenholm Road United Methodist Church.

Serves 8

2 (29-ounce) cans peach halves
1½ cups sugar
¾ cup apple cider vinegar
4 cinnamon sticks
2 teaspoons whole cloves

Drain peaches and reserve syrup. Combine sugar, vinegar, cinnamon, and cloves. Add syrup and bring to a boil. Simmer on low 10 minutes. Pour hot syrup over peaches. Cool and chill 4 hours before serving.

RICE, POTATOES, GRITS AND PASTA

Red Rice

Serves 8

3 slices thick-sliced bacon
2 cups chopped jumbo yellow onion
1 cup (from 28-ounce can) whole canned
   tomatoes, drained, chopped, and juice reserved
2⅔ cups tomato juice (made from reserved
   juice by adding enough water to make the
   2⅔ cups)
½ teaspoon sugar
1⅓ teaspoons salt

$\frac{1}{3}$ teaspoon black pepper
1 $\frac{1}{3}$ cups Uncle Ben's Converted® White Rice

3-quart saucepan
3-quart baking dish

Preheat oven to 350°.

Fry bacon in saucepan on low until brown, crumble, and return to fat. Increase heat to medium, and add onions to bacon and fat. Sauté, stirring occasionally, 5 minutes, or until onions are soft. Stir in tomatoes, juice, sugar, salt, and pepper. Bring to a boil, add rice, mix well, and pour into baking dish. Cover tightly with foil and bake at 350° for 1 hour, or until all liquid is absorbed. Fluff with fork and serve.

VEGETABLES

Broccoli

Serves 8

2 heads fresh broccoli (about 2 pounds)
2 quarts water
Pinch baking soda
2 teaspoons salt

3-gallon pot

Wash broccoli. Cut off florets, including tender parts of stem. Peel stalk and slice into $\frac{1}{2}$-inch pieces. Bring water, baking soda, and salt to a boil. Add broccoli and boil 5 minutes, or until fork easily pierces stem. Drain and serve, or rinse with cold water to stop cooking and set aside to use later.

Celery Amandine

This is one of many recipes Susan Boyd (Mrs. Darnall) of Columbia and Sapphire Lakes, N.C., has shared with us.

Serves 8

1 large stalk celery (4 cups cut celery)
2 Tablespoons butter
2 Tablespoons minced onion
4 cloves garlic, peeled and pressed
2 Tablespoons peeled and finely chopped fresh ginger
1 teaspoon chicken bouillon granules
$\frac{1}{4}$ cup slivered almonds, toasted

12-inch frying pan with lid

Divide stalk of celery, wash each piece, and cut diagonally into 2-inch lengths, approximately $\frac{1}{2}$-inch wide.

Heat butter in frying pan. Add onions, garlic, ginger, and bouillon granules and sauté on medium high, stirring occasionally, 5 minutes, or until onions and ginger are soft. Add celery and toss until mixed well. Reduce heat to low, cover pan, and cook 20 to 25 minutes, or until just tender. Stir often to prevent ginger from sticking to bottom of pan. Toss with toasted almonds and serve.

Peas and Mushrooms

Fresh green peas are rarely available. Before frozen peas, canned LeSueur® Peas were a staple in our pantry and bring back good memories of family meals during childhood. Two (16-ounce) bags of frozen peas, cooked by the directions on the package, can be substituted.

Serves 8

$\frac{1}{2}$ stick butter
2 garlic cloves, pressed
1 pound mushrooms, cleaned and quartered
1 teaspoon salt
$\frac{1}{2}$ teaspoon black pepper
2 (15-ounce) cans LeSueur® Early Peas or 2 (16-ounce) bags frozen peas cooked by directions on package

12-inch frying pan

Melt butter in frying pan on medium high. Add garlic, mushrooms, salt, and pepper. Sauté 5 minutes, or until mushrooms are tender and beginning to brown.

Rinse peas with cold water and drain. Add to mushrooms and toss to combine. Heat 3 to 5 minutes, or until peas are hot.

DESSERTS

Benne Seed Cookies

These are very thin, crunchy cookies. The recipe originated with Debbie Riker (Mrs. Tom), a fine cook from Columbia.

4 dozen (1½-inch)

1 egg white
½ cup light brown sugar
¼ teaspoon pure vanilla extract
2 Tablespoons butter, melted and at room temperature
Pinch salt
¼ cup all-purpose flour
½ Tablespoon finely chopped orange zest
¼ cup browned benne seeds (p.54)

Preheat oven to 325°. Line 2 baking sheets with aluminum foil and spray with vegetable spray.

Whip egg white in electric mixer on high until foamy. Add sugar and vanilla and stir by hand until well blended. Stir in butter, salt, flour, and orange zest and mix until well blended. Stir in browned benne seeds. Drop mixture onto baking sheets by half teaspoonfuls (about the size of a nickel). Bake at 325° for 8 to 10 minutes, or until golden brown. Remove sheet of foil with cookies on it and cool on foil. Start each batch on cool baking sheet. Freeze well.

Fresh Strawberry Cake

Alex's sister, Retta Miller, and her husband, Ronald, of Columbia gave us this recipe. It is a favorite during strawberry season.

Serves 12

CAKE
1 box high-quality white cake mix
1 Tablespoon self-rising flour
1 (3-ounce) package strawberry Jell-O®
¾ cup vegetable oil
½ cup water
½ cup strawberries (frozen or fresh, sliced and mixed with sugar to taste until juicy)
4 eggs

9 x 13 baking pan, greased and floured

ICING
1 stick butter, room temperature
1 (1-pound) box confectioners' sugar
½ cup strawberries (frozen or fresh, sliced)
6 whole strawberries for garnish

Serves 60

CAKE
3 boxes high-quality white cake mix
3 Tablespoons self-rising flour
3 (3-ounce) packages strawberry Jell-O®
2¼ cups vegetable oil
1½ cups water
1½ cups strawberries (frozen or fresh, sliced and mixed with sugar to taste until juicy)
12 eggs

18 x 26 baking sheet, greased and floured

ICING
3 sticks butter, room temperature
3 (1-pound) boxes confectioners' sugar
1½ cups strawberries (frozen or fresh, sliced)
30 whole strawberries for garnish

TO MAKE CAKE: Preheat regular oven to 350° or convection oven to 325°.

Combine cake mix, flour, Jell-O®, vegetable oil, water, and sugared strawberries in mixer (institutional, for large recipe). Add eggs one at a time and mix well after each. Pour in baking pan (or on sheet, for large recipe) and bake in either oven 25 to 30 minutes, or until cake is very brown and begins to pull away from sides of pan.

TO MAKE ICING: Beat butter and sift in sugar until both are well blended. Add strawberries and mix with the whipping attachment until smooth.

When cake is cool, smooth icing over top. Cut 3 x 4 (or 6 x 10 for 60). Slice reserved whole strawberries in half and place one on each piece of cake.

Key Lime Pie

Remember, Key Lime pies are not green; they are pale yellow. Green food coloring is a no-no.

Serves 8

CRUST
¾ cup graham cracker crumbs
  (about 6 graham crackers)
2½ Tablespoons sugar
½ stick butter, melted
1 egg white, lightly beaten

9-inch pie pan

FILLING
3 egg yolks (reserve whites)
1 (14-ounce) can Eagle® Brand Condensed
  Milk
½ cup fresh lime juice (reserve 1 teaspoon)
1 Tablespoon finely chopped lime zest

MERINGUE
3 egg whites
Pinch cream of tartar
6 Tablespoons sugar
Reserved teaspoon lime juice

TO MAKE CRUST: Preheat oven to 350°.
Mix graham cracker crumbs, sugar, and butter. Press into pie pan and brush with beaten egg white. Bake at 350° for 10 minutes, or until golden brown. Cool 5 minutes.

TO MAKE FILLING: Beat yolks in electric mixer 5 minutes, or until fluffy and light in color. Gradually whisk in condensed milk by hand. Reserve 1 teaspoon lime juice for meringue. Gradually whisk remaining lime juice into egg mixture until well blended. Whisk in lime zest.

TO MAKE MERINGUE: Whip egg whites in electric mixer on high until frothy. Add cream of tartar and reserved teaspoon of lime juice. Gradually add sugar and whip until whites are shiny and form soft peaks. Spoon meringue on top of pie filling in circles, starting from outside and covering pie crust.

Bake pie at 350° degrees for 15 minutes, or until meringue is lightly browned. Cool 15 minutes. Refrigerate 4 hours before slicing.

Peach Cobbler for 30

1⅓ (#10) cans peach pie filling
1 Tablespoon pure almond extract
1 Tablespoon cinnamon
5 cups blueberry muffin mix
  (from institutional-size bag)
2 sticks margarine, melted

11½ x 9 x 2½ pan sprayed with vegetable
  spray

Preheat convection oven to 350°.

Spread peach pie filling in pan. Chop whole slices of peaches in half. Add almond extract and cinnamon and mix with pie filling.

Cover top with blueberry muffin mix and drizzle with melted margarine. Bake at 350° for 15 minutes. Reduce to 325° and bake 15 minutes, or until filling is hot and bubbly and top is brown.

Pecan Pie

Lee Godbey makes the best pecan pie ever, and this is his recipe.

Serves 8

1 (9-inch) Easy Pie Crust, unbaked (p.37)

3 eggs
½ packed cup light brown sugar
1 cup light corn syrup
½ stick butter, melted
1 teaspoon pure vanilla extract
1 ½ cups pecan pieces or halves
Soft Whipped Cream (p.58)

Preheat oven to 350°.

Combine eggs and sugar in electric mixer. Beat in corn syrup, butter, and vanilla. Place pecans in crust and pour batter over. Bake at 350° for 50 to 55 minutes, or until top is brown and center is firm when shaken. Cool to room temperature before slicing, but don't refrigerate. Serve each slice with a dollop of softly whipped cream.

NOTE: Pecan pieces make a pie easier to cut, but pecan halves make it more elegant.

Sugar Cookies

This recipe is one that we traditionally use for Valentine's Day cookies. We use a 2½-inch heart-shaped cutter and sprinkle them with red "sprinkles." However, this is a great recipe for all cookie cutters.

3 dozen (2½-inch) cookies

1 stick butter, room temperature
1 cup sugar
1 egg
1 Tablespoon milk
½ teaspoon pure vanilla extract
Red food coloring (optional)

1 ¾ cups all-purpose flour
2 teaspoons baking powder
½ teaspoon salt
6 Tablespoons red "sprinkles"

Cream butter in electric mixer. Gradually add sugar and beat until light and fluffy. Add egg and beat well. Add milk and vanilla and beat well. If desired, add enough red food coloring to turn dough red. Combine flour, baking powder, and salt and mix well. Add to butter mixture ¼ cup at a time, mixing well until each cup is totally absorbed. Cover dough and refrigerate 8 hours.

When ready to bake cookies, preheat oven to 350°. Spray baking sheets with vegetable spray. Scoop out about a sixth of the dough and roll it out about ¼-inch thick, or as thin as possible, using as much flour as necessary. Cut out hearts and sprinkle with red "sprinkles." Place on baking sheets and repeat with remaining dough. Bake at 350° for 12 minutes, or until lightly browned. Cool on baking sheets.

NOTE: If making a large recipe, bake in a convection oven at 325° for about 4 minutes, or until lightly browned.

A silver basket, c. 1900, with Wadmalaw Island strawberries

Guide to Illustrations

The College of Charleston Campus is composed of more than 100 architecturally and historically significant buildings that have been restored for use as classrooms, faculty and administrative offices, student housing, fraternity and sorority houses, and centers for recreation and social events. These historic buildings, some grand and imposing, others following the vernacular styles of the Lowcountry, represent more than 200 years of architectural history. They are set amid a honeycomb of walled gardens and lush vegetation that makes the College of Charleston one of the most distinguished urban campuses in America.

Cover Image & Pages 16-17
Randolph Hall, 66 George Street, ca. 1828.
This graceful and distinguished structure has served continuously as a center of campus activities since its construction more than 150 years ago. Randolph Hall was named for Dr. Harrison Randolph, President of the College for almost 50 years beginning in 1897. The central portion of the main structure was built in 1828. Additions made in the 1850s and in this century have brought the building to its present form.

Frontispiece & Pages 56-57, 61
Dining Room, The President's House, 6 Glebe Street, ca. 1770.
Built in 1770 as a new parsonage for St. Philip's Parish by the rector, Dr. Robert Smith, on glebe lands donated to the church by Mrs. Affra Coming. The term "glebe" refers to lands given to the church for its support. The church owned "The Bishop Robert Smith House" until 1961 when the College purchased and restored this handsome house to its original design. During the past 228 years, Six Glebe Street has housed many ordinary and extraordinary tenants. Among those have been a Governor, a United States Senator, an Episcopal Bishop, two Rectors of St. Philip's

Church, a Chief Justice of the United States Supreme Court, a Chief Judge of the South Carolina Court of Appeals and six of the nineteen Presidents of the College of Charleston. The portrait over the mantle is of Edward Whittingham Thomas, Alex's ancestor who graduated from the College in 1851.

The Drawing Room.
Decorated for the Holidays with a 12-foot tree using relief clay ornaments with gold glazes and stained glass hand made by Del Dutrow. The ornaments represent many holiday traditions from cultures around the world. Hot chocolate in an antique Imari cocoa pot, cookies in Victorian silver baskets, and punch in a Victorian cut crystal punch bowl are sweet treats for friends, faculty and students before the holidays begin.

Page xviii
Porter's Lodge, principal entrance to Randolph Hall, George Street, ca. 1850s.
A southern-style continental breakfast in the Craig Cafeteria Courtyard with a view of Porter's Lodge. This classically inspired building provides an elegant and somewhat triumphant approach to the grounds of Randolph Hall.

Page 5
The William Blacklock House, 18 Bull Street, ca. 1800.
Considered one of the finest Adamesque style buildings in America and designated as a National Historic Landmark, the Blacklock House contains notable interior ornamentation and a graceful circular stair rising to the second floor. The facade is distinguished by its double flight of stairs with iron rails and elegant iron tracery in the transom, fanlight and sidelights. The house is used for lunch and dinner meetings, college receptions and wedding receptions. The garden, including the Pierrine Byrd Rose Garden, is a source of

most of the cut flowers used on the campus. This house and others were purchased and donated to the College by Richard Hampton Jenrette.

Page 1
Dining Room, The William Blacklock House.
The wide front hall, the parlor, and the entrance to the music room can be seen along with the formal dinner setting in the dining room.

Page 9
The Sottile Theater, George Street at King Street, ca. 1855, remodeled 1923 & 1992.
When this theater was remodeled in the 1920s by Mr. Albert Sottile, it became the largest in the state, seating over 2,000 people. Originally the Gloria Theater, the name was changed in 1989 by the College to honor Mr. Sottile and his family, who have taken a major interest in the preservation and renovation of the building. It now serves as a site for the University of Charleston commencement, student and parent assemblies, theatrical and musical performances, Spoleto presentations, and the Film festival.

Pages 6-7
Interior, The Sottile Theater.
Receptions before and after performances in Sottile Theater are held in the second floor lobby with a balcony overlooking George Street. A silver "supper service," ca. 1900, offers pecans, shrimp, open-faced sandwiches, fruit and sauces with a tureen filled with dahlias as a centerpiece.

Pages 10-11
Remley's Point, on the Wando River.
The Cougar Club, named for our athletic mascot, has parties before and after the games at Remley's Point on the Wando River. The nationally ranked men's soccer team was one win away from the NCAA Final Four in 1994. The men's and women's golf programs contin-

ue to be among the region's elite, consistently registering top ten finishes. The women's basketball team had the 24th highest team GPA among women's basketball teams in 1997. Both the men's and women's swimming squads received Academic All-American recognition. The women's tennis team received a regional ranking of ninth in the Southeast last season and 68th in the nation. The men's tennis team is an Academic All-American team and one player is a two-time All-Conference team member. Our equestrian team ranked 2nd in the nation twice and for the past 15 years has consistently ranked in the top six. Relatively new teams in baseball, volleyball, women's soccer, softball, and cross-country continue to advance.

Page 21
Interior, Randolph Hall.
Alumni Hall, located in Randolph Hall, served as the Chapel and the assembly room for the entire student body until recent years. Dinners for as many as 100 can be served, with a stage for speakers and entertainment.

Pages 22-23, 27
Dixie Plantation.
Dixie Plantation on the Stono River, with a splendid double avenue of oaks, was the home of John Henry Dick, a popular and well-known artist, author, photographer, and ornithologist. He left 816 acres of woods, fresh water ponds, and marsh on the inland waterway to the College for educational purposes. Dixie is being used by various departments, including biology, geology, and the School of the Arts. Small academic retreats and meetings of up to 50 people can be held in the 1947 house. Large dinners, picnics and receptions are held on the banks of the river.

Page 33
The Cistern, ca. 1857, Towell Library, ca. 1856, and Randolph Hall, ca. 1826-1856, George Street.
For almost two centuries this area represented

the entire campus of the College and is now designated as a National Historic Landmark. The Cistern, a popular landmark and meeting place, originally functioned as the receptacle for the campus water supply. Today it serves as the ceremonial heart of the campus and the setting for graduation ceremonies, music and dance performances, alumni receptions, and the popular Parents Weekend every fall. Towell Library now serves as the Admissions Office.

Pages 40-41
Interior, Randolph Hall, Board Room.
A portrait of Dr. Moultrie Rutledge Rivers, a 1890 graduate of the College and President of the Board of Trustees from 1925 until 1940, hangs over the sideboard in the boardroom in Randolph Hall. Lunch is served on Canton china, ca. 1800.

Pages 44-45, 49
Caroline and Albert Simons, Jr. Center for Historic Preservation Program, 12 Bull Street, ca. 1851.
Known historically as the Hugh P. Cameron House, this two-storied structure with classic Charleston piazzas was built in the decade before the Civil War and remodeled in 1892 to reflect the Colonial Revival and late Victorian style.

Interior.
The Preservation Center is being used by students as a studio classroom for preservation planning and urban and architectural design by day and a dinner and reception area by night. The portrait is of Caroline Mitchell Simons before she became a student at the College.

Pages 50-51
Interior, The President's House, the Dining Room.
The portrait over the sideboard is of John Zacariah Sicgling, 1791-1867, whose many descendants include College graduates,

patrons and faculty members. He established the first music house in America on Broad Street in 1819 and imported the first harp to America. The antique china is a Wedgwood pattern. Alex is a descendant of Judge Theodore Gaillard, 1766-1829, whose portrait at the age of nine is at the end of the room.

Pages 62-63
Interior, The President's House, the Garden Room.
The first students at the College were kept warm by two huge fireplaces in what is now called the Garden Room. There are 10 fireplaces in the house. The room will seat 60 for lunch or dinner with space for a speaker and entertainment.

Pages 66-67
Willard A. Silcox Gymnasium, George Street.
With holiday lights, candles, and a crystal ball the Willard Silcox Gym is magically transformed for a Faculty and Staff Holiday Dinner Dance for a thousand.

Pages 72-73
Kitchen, The President's House, on New Year's Day.
Pet canary "Neil Diamond" watches as Alex and Zoe Sanders sip oyster stew before eating a traditional meal of Collards and Hoppin John to assure prosperity and good luck in the new year.

Pages 78-79
The Faculty House, 20 Glebe Street, ca. 1846.
Historically known as the Thompson-Muller House, ca. 1846, provides an historic setting for faculty sponsored events. The "single" house was built by George Thompson on land leased from the church which was called "glebe lands." In 1879, Mrs. Christiana Durkopp Krusse bought the house and purchased the land from the church making it the first lot to break the glebe. The College purchased the house from the Muller family,

descendants of Mrs. Krusse, in 1971. The Japanese Magnolia makes a spectacular display in February. The English Department is next door.

Pages 82-83
Interior, The Faculty House.
The Faculty House dining room displays retired professors' portraits. The chandelier is original to the dining room and was donated by Jan Muller Goin (Mrs. David).

Pages 88-89
Interior, The President's House.
The College collections include antique porcelain, portraits, furnishings and other works of fine art that are on loan or have been donated by friends and alumni of the College. The Spode tea set in the library was made in the early 1800s in the tobacco leaf pattern and is typical of the rich traditions in the Lowcountry. For the donors' celebration, more than five hundred guests are entertained by musicians from the School of the Arts on three floors while guests move from floor to floor and room to room for a variety of foods and beverages.

Pages 100-101
Charleston Harbor.
A morning sailing class in the harbor with the historic East Battery in the background. The sailing team won the 1997-1998 Fowle Trophy for best all-around college sailing team in America.

Pages 112-113
Interior, The President's House.
The Garden Room at Six Glebe housed a boys' academy which was started by Bishop Robert Smith and was the beginning of the public education program at the College of Charleston. Dr. Smith's portrait hangs over the piano. He was the first President of the College and became the first Episcopal Bishop of South Carolina.

Pages 118-119, 123
The Avery Normal Institute and Research Center for African-American History and Culture, 125 Bull Street, ca. 1868.
Built to serve as the first secondary school for African-Americans in our nation's history. The third floor exhibit gallery will accommodate 200 for formal and informal dinners and seminars. Antique chandeliers with lighted candles hang from the high ceilings.

Page 129
The Sottile House, 11 College Street, ca. 1890.
The Sottile House, built in the Queen Anne style of architecture, was acquired through the generosity of the descendants of the Albert Sottile family in 1964. Once used as a dormitory, it now houses the College of Charleston Foundation and the Alumni Association.

Pages 124-125
Interior, The Sottile House.
The original dining room now serves as the Foundation Board Room where many lunches and meetings are held. The silver, china, linens, and crystal are all family heirlooms once used in this room by the Sottile family and now belong to Joyce Long Darby (Mrs. Charles P.) and Mary Ellen Long Way (Mrs. Charles S., Jr.), daughters of Mrs. Albert Sottile Long (1905-1996) whose portrait is shown when she was four years old.

Pages 130-131
The Tate Center.
The Tate Center for Entrepreneurship was the first entrepreneurship center in the state. Jack Tate, founder of Baby Superstore, Inc., donated the funds to complete the building. As the newest addition to the College of Charleston campus, the Tate Center was completed and dedicated in April 1998. The beautiful Tate Center Gallery and reception area can be seen with the portrait of Jack Tate by Del Dutrow.

Index

HORS d'OEUVRE

Asparagus, 107
Boiled Creek Shrimp, 8
Boiled Peanuts, 12
Cheese Wafers with Benne Seeds, 120
Chicken Salad Sandwiches, 111
College Cheese Wafers, 110
Crab Cakes, 93
Cream Cheese and Olive Spread or Dip, 111
Fresh Artichokes with Hollandaise, 94
Fried Okra, 38
Fried Oysters, 132
Marinated Shrimp, 93
Melba Toast, 18
Open-Faced Cucumber Sandwiches, 8
Open-Faced Tomato Sandwiches, 8
Pimiento Cheese, 103
Potatoes with Sour Cream and Caviar, 132
Sautéed Quail Breasts, 120
Shrimp Salad Sandwiches, 110
Sleeping Shrimp, 90
Toasted Pecans, 9
Toasted Saltines, 141

APPETIZERS

Broccoli Soup, 134
Cantaloupe and Prosciutto, 132
College Oysters, 52
Corn Chowder, 18
Crab Cakes, 93
Crab Salad, 2
Marinated Shrimp, 93
Onion Soup with Croutons, 46
Oyster Stew, 74
Randolph Hall Crab Soup, 106
Tomato Aspic, 133

SALADS

Avocado and Grapefruit Salad, 36
Cantaloupe, Tomato, Cucumber, and Mint Salad, 115
Cranberry Salad, 133
Fresh Pineapple Salad, 36
Fruit Salad Dressing, 36
Marinated Shrimp, 93
Marinated Sweet Slaw, 12
Preservation Salad, 46
Slaw, 25
Summer Tomato Salad, 126
Sunrise Grapefruit Salad, 42
Tomato Aspic, 133

SOUPS

Broccoli Soup, 134
Corn Chowder, 18
Craig Cafeteria Clam Chowder, 134
Onion Soup with Croutons, 46
Oyster Stew, 74
Randolph Hall Crab Soup, 106

ENTREES

SEAFOOD

Barbecued Shrimp, 24
Boiled Shrimp: Two Methods, 135
Crab Cakes, 93
College Shrimp, 120
Deviled Crab, 126
Fried Oysters, 132
Lowcountry Shrimp and Crab Boil, 13
Oven-Poached Salmon and Leeks, 19
Oyster Pie, 84
Oyster Stew, 74
Randolph Hall Crab Soup, 106
Sautéed Flounder, 135

Shrimp and Gravy, 80
Shrimp and Orzo, 115
Shrimp Creole, 136
Shrimp Salad, 137
Steamed Oysters, 137

MEAT

Beef Filets, 47
College of Charleston "Mystery Meat," 30
Country Ham, 36
Crown Roast of Pork with Cranberry Dressing, 52
Grilled Tenderloin, 91
Oven-Roasted Tenderloin, 92
Roasted Pork Loin, 74
Round Table Grilled Veal Chops, 2
Spoleto Lamb Chops, 114

POULTRY

Baked Chicken, 138
Chicken Salad, 138
College Chicken and Broccoli Gratin, 64
College Chicken Bog, 139
College of Charleston Quail, 24
Cornish Hens, 106
Duck à l'Orange, 84
Fried Quail, 114
Prizewinning Quail Stew, 42
Turkey and Corn Bread Dressing Cakes, 92

BREADS AND PASTRY

College Biscuits, 3
College Cheese Wafers, 110
Dixie Plantation Yeast Rolls, 25
Easy Pie Crust, 37
French Bread, 139
Homemade Loaf Bread, 102
Melba Toast, 18
Remley's Point Corn Bread Muffins, 14
Skillet Corn Bread, 14
Sour Cream Muffins, 140
Spoon Bread, 85

CONDIMENTS AND SAUCES

Amaretto Fruit Sauce, 9
Apple Plum Chutney, 114
Applesauce with Horseradish, 76
Béarnaise Sauce, 47
Caramel Dip for Apples, 141
Chocolate Sauce, 9
Crab Cake Sauce, 141

Dill Sauce, 142
Fruit Salad Dressing, 36
Hollandaise Sauce, 94
Homemade Horseradish Sauce, 92
Homemade Mayonnaise, 127
Homemade Tartar Sauce, 142
Mayonnaise Sauce, 8
Orange-Brandy Sauce, 55
Pesto, 90
Pickled Peaches, 106
Raspberry Sauce, 4
Vanilla Fruit Sauce, 9
Wando Cocktail Sauce, 13

RICE, POTATOES, GRITS, AND PASTA

Brown Rice, 26,
Mashed Potatoes, 31
Red Rice, 142
Rice, 31
Roasted New Potatoes, 19
Scalloped Potatoes, 2
Spoon Bread, 85
Stone-Ground Grits, 80
Twice-Baked Stand Up Potatoes, 47
Whipped Sweet Potatoes, 75
Wild and Brown Rice, 54
Wild Rice with Mushrooms, 54

VEGETABLES

Asparagus, 107
Broccoli, 143
Butter Beans, 121
Celery Amandine, 143
Collards with Chops, 75
Fried Okra, 38
Hoppin' John, 74
Green Beans with Benne Seeds, 54
Peas and Mushrooms, 143
Pole Beans, 43
Ridgeway Squash Casserole, 126
Sautéed Mushrooms, 48
Sautéed Spinach, 3
Sautéed Spinach and Leeks, 3
Stewed Corn, 126
Summer Tomato Pie, 36
Tomatoes Stuffed with Feta Cheese, 121
Winter Tomato Pie, 37

BEVERAGES

Amaretto Hot Chocolate, 58
Cranberry-Apple Holiday Punch, 58

Graduation Punch, 110
Homemade Lemonade, 15

SWEETS

Benne Seed Cookies, 144
Brownies, 68
Chocolate-Covered Cherries, 95
Chocolate Fudge Cookies, 59
Chocolate Peanut Butter Cookies, 60
Fresh Strawberry Cake, 144
Ginger Cookies, 58
Gingered Fruit Compote, 98
Holiday Butter Cookies, 59
Lemon Squares, 71
Orange Mousse, 98
Peanut Butter and Jelly Sandwiches, 12
Pecan Sandies, 20
Sandies, 20
Sugar Cookies, 146

DESSERTS

Apple Pie, 76
Blueberry Pie, 116
Chocolate Pie, 85
Chocolate Sauce, 9
Cream Cheese Pie, 48
Cream Cheese Pound Cake, 70
Custard, 70
Equestrian Team Apple Spice Cake, 38
Fresh Strawberry Cake, 144
Gingerbread, 64
Gingered Fruit Compote, 98
Key Lime Pie, 145
Lemon Chess Pie, 122
Lemon Mousse with Lemon Curd, 20
Lemon Sauce, 65
Orange-Brandy Sauce, 55
Parents Weekend Persimmon Cake, 32
Peach Pie, 127
Pecan Pie, 146
Raspberry Sauce, 4
Raspberry Trifle, 68
Rum Pie, 107
Soft Whipped Cream, 58
Swedish Cream, 4
Winter Fruit Torte, 26

SHORTCUTS

Gingerbread for 96, 65
Shortcut Pickled Peaches, 142
Shortcut Raspberry Trifle, 70

RECIPES FOR THE MULTITUDES

Apple Crisp for 120, 32
Artichoke Pickle makes 12 pints, 127
Barbecued Pig for 60 to 75, 30
Battery Chocolate Chip Cookies makes 12 dozen, 103
Cheese Torta for 50, 90
Cheese Wafers makes 6 dozen, 120
Chocolate Fudge Cookies makes 33 dozen, 59
Chocolate Peanut Butter Cookies makes 5 dozen, 60
College Pâté for 50, 90
Corn Bread Dressing Cakes for 60, 92
Corn Bread for 120, 15
Corn Chowder for 150, 18
Craig Cafeteria Clam Chowder for 100, 134
Cranberry-Apple Holiday Punch for 200, 58
Cranberry Salad for 150, 133
Cream Cheese Pie for 168, 48
Fresh Strawberry Cake for 50, 144
Gingerbread for 96, 65
Ginger Cookies makes 54 dozen, 58
Graduation Punch for 50 (4-ounce servings), 110
Lemon Chess Pie for 160, 122
Lemon Sauce for 96, 65
Lemon Stickies makes 16 dozen, 15
Peach Cobbler for 30, 145
Seasoned Oyster Crackers for 20, 12
Shrimp Creole for 50, 136
Slaw for 180, 25
Steamed Oysters, 137
Sunrise Grapefruit Salad for 32, 42
Raspberry Trifle (Shortcut) for 30, 70
Winter Tomato Pie for 80, 37

BREAKFAST

Coffee Cake, 81
Country Ham, 36
Mushroom Strata, 80
Shrimp and Gravy, 80

Designed by Sally Heineman

155